SELF-PORTRAIT WITH A SWARM OF BEES

JAN WAGNER

SELF-PORTRAIT WITH A SWARM OF BEES
SELECTED POEMS

Translated by
Iain Galbraith
& introduced by
Karen Leeder

2015

Published by Arc Publications,
Nanholme Mill, Shaw Wood Road
Todmorden OL14 6DA, UK
www.arcpublications.co.uk

Translation copyright © Iain Galbraith 2015
Translator's Preface copyright © Iain Galbraith 2015
Introduction copyright © Karen Leeder 2015
Copyright in the present edition © Arc Publications 2015

978 1908376 82 4 (pbk)
978 1908376 83 1 (hbk)
978 1908376 84 8 (ebook)

ACKNOWLEDGEMENTS
'champignons', 'des toten lenins reise nach tjumen', 'fenchel'
and 'frösche' from *Probebohrung im Himmel* (2001)
© Jan Wagner 2001 / 2015

'giersch', 'versuch über mücken', ein pferd',
'das weidenkätzchen', 'grottenolm', 'laken', im brunnen' and
'selbstporträt mit bienenschwarm' from
Regentonnenvariationen © Hanser Berlin im Carl Hanser Verlag, 2014

and poems from:
Guerickes Sperling
© 2004 Berlin Verlag in der Piper Verlag GmbH, Berlin
Achtzehn Pasteten
© 2007 Berlin Verlag in der Piper Verlag GmbH, Berlin
Australien
© 2010 Berlin Verlag in der Piper Verlag GmbH, Berlin

The translation of this work was supported by a grant from the Goethe-Institut which is funded by the German Ministry of Foreign Affairs.

Design by Tony Ward
Cover design: Tony Ward & Ben Styles
Printed in Great Britain by
TJ International, Padstow, Cornwall

This book is in copyright. Subject to statutory exception and to provision of relevant collective licensing agreements, no reproduction of any part of this book may take place without the written permission of Arc Publications.

'Visible Poets'
Series Editor: Jean Boase-Beier

CONTENTS

Series Editor's Note / 7
Translator's Preface / 9
Introduction / 18

26 / champignons • mushrooms / 27
28 / des toten lenins reise • dead lenin's journey
nach tjumen   to tyumen / 29
32 / fenchel • fennel / 33
34 / frösche • frogs / 35
36 / guerickes sperling • guericke's sparrow / 37
38 / weihnachten in • christmas in
huntsville, texas   huntsville, texas / 39
40 / kleinstadtelegie • small town elegy / 41
42 / der veteranengarten • the veterans' garden / 43
46 / smithfield market • smithfield market / 47
48 / regenwürmer • earthworms / 49
50 / kolumbus • columbus / 51
52 / störtebeker • störtebeker / 53
54/ der mann aus dem meer • the man from the sea / 55
56 / dobermann • dobermann / 57
58 / quallen • jellyfish / 59
62 / dezember 1914 • december 1914 / 63
64 / anomalien • anomalies / 65
66 / shepherds' pie • shepherd's pie / 67
68 / pâté chaud de harengs • pâté chaud de harengs aux
aux pommes de terre   pommes de terre / 69
70 / cheese and onion pasties • cheese and onion pasties / 71
72 / quittenpastete • quince jelly / 73
74 / der westen • the west / 75
76 / staniszów • staniszów / 77
78 / teebeutel • tea-bag / 79
80 / chamäleon   chameleon / 81

82 / historien: onesilos • histories: onesilos / 83
84 / gecko • gecko / 85
86 / von den ölbäumen • concerning the olive trees / 87
92 / amisch • amish / 93
94 / elegie für knievel • elegy for knievel / 95
96 / der wassermann • the merman / 97
98 / steinway • steinway / 99
100 / wippe • see-saw / 101
102 / meteorit • meteorite / 103
104 / australien • australia / 105
108 / giersch • bindweed / 109
110 / versuch über mücken • essay on midges / 111
112 / ein pferd • a horse / 113
116 / das weidenkätzchen • the catkin / 117
118 / grottenolm • olm / 119
122 / laken • sheets / 123
124 / im brunnen • in the well / 125
126 / selbstporträt mit • self-portrait with a swarm
bienenschwarm   of bees / 127

Biographical notes / 128

SERIES EDITOR'S NOTE

The 'Visible Poets' series was established in 2000, and set out to challenge the view that translated poetry could or should be read without regard to the process of translation it had undergone. Since then, things have moved on. Today there is more translated poetry available and more debate on its nature, its status, and its relation to its original. We know that translated poetry is neither English poetry that has mysteriously arisen from a hidden foreign source, nor is it foreign poetry that has silently rewritten itself in English. We are more aware that translation lies at the heart of all our cultural exchange; without it, we must remain artistically and intellectually insular.

One of the aims of the series was, and still is, to enrich our poetry with the very best work that has appeared elsewhere in the world. And the poetry-reading public is now more aware than it was at the start of this century that translation cannot simply be done by anyone with two languages. The translation of poetry is a creative act, and translated poetry stands or falls on the strength of the poet-translator's art. For this reason 'Visible Poets' publishes only the work of the best translators, and gives each of them space, in a Preface, to talk about the trials and pleasures of their work.

From the start, 'Visible Poets' books have been bilingual. Many readers will not speak the languages of the original poetry but they, too, are invited to compare the look and shape of the English poems with the originals. Those who can are encouraged to read both. Translation and original are presented side-by-side because translations do not displace the originals; they shed new light on them and are in turn themselves illuminated by the presence of their source poems. By drawing the readers' attention to the act of translation itself, it is the aim of these books to make the work of both the original poets and their translators more visible.

Jean Boase-Beier

TRANSLATOR'S PREFACE

Many years can pass between first looking into a 'foreign' poet's work and the appearance of a book that will document the translator's full engagement. But where does the translation itself begin? Perhaps there is a moment of 'first love', when a translator feels almost ineluctably drawn to a quality that is at once alluringly other and yet also hauntingly close – a distinctive tone of voice, perhaps, or a more than likeable subtlety of attention. "Something seemed to click", we might later recall – a recognizable moment of quickening along the *arculate fasciculus*, the neural loop which scientists hold to be the site of our written and spoken language experience. And perhaps that thrilling early moment of heightened focus is necessary to throw open the doors to a deeper, more purposeful, and also more accountable kind of reading.

A translator's reading – a reading or seeking *for* the object of translation – does not only pursue the usual, inward, connotative and cognitive pleasures that derive from transforming a unique distribution of script into sensation, representation, association, and idea. Unstilled by these gratifications alone, or, who knows, lacking the necessary autonomy to let the euphoria simply burn and fade, the translator will follow his or her insight, empathy, admiration and rapture, but also any number of less well advertised, yet equally powerful emotions – envy, rivalry or even anger (Laura Riding's "rugged black of anger" which has "an uncertain smile border") – to a risky, impossible, poetic head. What I mean is the task of facing the 'source' text on its own terms and sharing the reading experience in the target language. But also, crucially and in apparent contradiction to that 'selfless' service, the presumption of rebuilding the 'foreign' poem on the translator's own terms and ground, bound in the target language by the constraints and demands that emanate from his or her own time and place. Thus the origin of a translated text is always dual in character, and the territory between its sources debatable.

When I speak of 'facing' the poem 'on its own terms', for example – might I really be facing it down? When I say 'sharing' – do I actually mean appropriating, incorporating, cannibalizing? And when I say 'rebuilding' – should the process I am describing more properly be called an 'un-building', piece by piece, an obliterating, a robbing of stones for my own building project? Finding the knife-edge which an ambitious translation – one that attempts to fulfil the demands of both poem and reader – will always feel keenly, a translator is never permitted to forget the duality of his or her position: it is Janus-faced, with an abyss at either side of the knife-blade. In the teeth of all that is obvious and yet oddly invisible – the absence in a translation of any word the 'foreign' text once contained – both the poem and its reader (i.e. of the translation) will generally hope for the same thing: "A tune beyond us as we are, / But nothing changed by the blue guitar". Like the translator, the guitarist in Wallace Stevens's poem 'The Man with the Blue Guitar' must serve and satisfy two masters, and his worldly knowledge of the way things change on the strings of a "blue guitar" does not diminish his accountability to both patrons. But again and again, in more inward moments, he returns to an apparent paradox, an unsettling mystery, one of the Muse-questions of guitarists, poets and translators alike:

> Where
> Do I begin and end? And where
>
> As I strum the thing, do I pick up
> That which momentously declares
>
> Itself not to be I and yet
> Must be. It could be nothing else.[1]

The poetics of translation inevitably entail much that will never be explained, or at least always explained differently. Perhaps because I am a slow reader, too, I invariably need a considerable time to work through these complexities and taboos in my effort to read productively, as a translator undoubtedly should, beyond the elation and fuzzy matching of the initial encounter: reading over time and through a language, reading for the primal syntax.

*

I first met Jan Wagner in January 2001 when we both attended a 'literary' gathering hosted by the British Council in Cologne. The date is significant for two reasons. Firstly, it was shortly before the young German poet published his first volume of poems, *Probebohrung im Himmel* (Test Drill in the Sky), and secondly because he was still, until 2003, the editor, together with Thomas Girst, of an especially eye-catching literary periodical, *Die Außenseite des Elements* (The Outside of the Element). I remember the poet showing this 'object' to little groups of guests at a drinks reception, and when I walked over to ask him what kind of magazine it was, he held up a box, which I supposed must contain several copies. However, on closer inspection, it turned out to be the thing itself with the title and latest issue number emblazoned on its otherwise plain exterior. With a mischievous twinkle in his eye Jan Wagner tentatively lifted the lid of the box – and it was as if he were about to reveal a clutch of eggs, or a frog, or maybe some outrageous noise. Inside was a collection of loose leaves – poems, photographs, artworks, stories, essays and other literary items, some 100 in number, by artists and writers from different countries. It was a lovely thing, and a big hit at the reception. Later I learned that the idea went back to Marcel Duchamp's

'Bôite-en-valise' and other experiments with the 'musée portatif'. Within minutes we were talking about poetry and poets – those in or outside the box. It soon emerged that Jan was an aficionado of Anglo-American poetry, a former student at Trinity College, Dublin, and the translator of poems by Charles Simic (he has since translated volumes by James Tate, Matthew Sweeney, Simon Armitage, and others). Within an hour or so he had handed me the proofs for *Probebohrung im Himmel*, one of the first, or possibly *the* first book of poems to appear from the still relatively new Berlin Verlag (founded in 1995). I promised to read the book overnight, and did so. It was an impressive début, and immediately kindled my readiness to engage. Another three years would pass, however, before I began translating Jan Wagner's poetry.

Oddly, the incident with Jan's quizzical 'box' of loose leaves has remained in my mind for a reason that has less to do with its contents than its name. As I came to translate his work, initially for the 2004 Rotterdam International Poetry Festival and over the years since then, I came to think of Jan Wagner's "boxes" almost as if they prefigured, in some mysterious way, the poems I was translating. Typically for me, as time passed, I began to forget the name of the periodical, and to replace it with my own versions of its conundrum: "the outside of the inside of the surface", or "the inside of the outside of the poem" – was not that, I asked myself, exactly what I was trying to fathom? Later, Jan told me that the phrase 'Außenseite des Elements' had originated in the building trade. It can be read on stickers attached to identify the outward surfaces of windows, timber laminae, door leaves, wooden or plastic flaps, and other 'ready' elements.

The idea of construction, of inner workings and moveable, integrated surfaces, occupied my mind again and again while working on versions of Jan Wagner's poems. My translations were encounters with the inner workings of the element – or dimension – of poetry. It became clear that I was dealing with poetic machines: sonnets, sestinas, Sapphics, syllabics. Indeed, machines and instruments of various types (for example in the poem 'guericke's sparrow' p. 37), as well as other intricate inorganic and especially organic objects (mushrooms, fennel, worms, pasties), often feature in Jan Wagner's work. A poem, we might hazard, is a highly sophisticated instrument for the measurement of, and ingress to, the real in all its dimensions. A poem is a kind of chip, or in the poet's own view: "A good poem can combine the maximum of linguistic resources in the smallest of fields, harmonizing opposites and paradoxes, allowing them to chime, amplifying musicality and meaning." In Wagner's case I should emphasize that the poems are not only elaborate, cunning, and worldly, but genuinely entertaining. Indeed, without our capacity for enjoyment, if I understand the tenor of Wagner's aesthetic communion, reality would remain elusive. He is, as one German critic (Thomas Steinfeld) has put it, "a past master of delight".

*

Typically, Jan Wagner's poems show an unerring instinct for the surprising perspective on events or commonplace objects (plants, animals, landscapes), as well as a kind of impish relish in absurd detail and precarious balance. He is undoubtedly one of the most skilful contemporary German poets, confronting his translator with a challenging array of poetic forms. I have already mentioned sonnets, sestinas, Sapphics and syllabics, but over the years I have also 'faced' villanelles, haikus and rondeaux, as well as several varieties of rhyme. Wagner is a vigilant yet playful chronicler of the quotidian, his meticulous handling of image and sound forging a sensuous, almost luminous palpability. Intensely curious, constantly attentive to the unanticipated possibilities afforded by the corset of metre and form, his poems are primarily an exploratory celebration of what he has called poetry's "bond with our steaming, glowing, odorous, noisy world".

It need hardly be said that any poet who demonstrates such a talent for working with traditional forms – and Wagner's motives for doing so are experimentalist and adventurous rather than sentimental or fogyish – will bring a 'box' of riddles to the translator's table. Such difficulties have, on occasion, stopped me in my tracks. Stopped? Is one truly motionless when reflecting on method? Wagner himself has a refreshing take on the "formal corset". His point is not that the rules were made to be broken, but that we should conceive of them "less in terms of an obligation than as a process encouraging the imagery and thought of a poem to set out in a new or unanticipated direction". A poem, he says, will "uphold the fundamental poetic virtues of surprise and transgression (whether in violating conventions of its own making or rules imposed from without), granting the greatest possible freedom in the most compact space". Listening to his rhymes, for example, we notice that they are rarely perfect or pure. He has, it seems to me, an Epicurean respect for the (apparently) chance correspondence of vowels, the unpredictable 'swerve' of word-particles – Lucretius's "clinamen". In copying that last word from a handwritten note I myself suffered a kind of swerve, and at first read 'chinaman', itself an apt metaphor for the Wagnerian rhyme: a kind of left-armed spun version of the 'googly'.[2] For sometimes his rhymes are canny enough to persuade you they aren't there at all – assonant eighths and tenths rather than half-rhymes. And is it only my imagination – or is it true that, given the right context, two words entirely lacking in homophonic relation can nonetheless stage a rhyme? Wagner's schemes promote a modern euphony, in which cohesion is by no means absent, but where sense can be fragmentary and rhyme imperfect, forced, off, dirty, skewed. Rhyme, we learn, is no simple substance, and the sound patterns in a poem can produce different kinds of translational difficulty. To exit by way of an entry, here are four types of difficulty – two of them instances of different kinds of phonetic impasse – faced by the translator of the present book.

Take the poem 'giersch' (p. 108). A glance at the German text – even for someone who cannot understand what he or she is reading – reveals how the poem develops its increasingly proliferous sound-patterns from the vowels and consonants of the title-word itself. Now, 'giersch' is ground elder, and it will be seen that the relentless rhizomic cascade of its "ie" and "sch"-sounds from line to line eventually suffocates all other sound in the poem, mirroring the typical spread of this plant in a garden. Although there are alternative English names for ground elder, none, I thought, offered a sonorous potential equivalent to 'giersch'. At first then, I considered the poem beyond translation, but adopting the libertarian ethos of Jan Wagner's pursuit of swerve – the "new or unanticipated direction" – I have wilfully and freely switched gardens to select a different blossoming perennial smotherer – the equally troublesome and rampantly convolving 'bindweed' – seeking to develop an internally rhyming experience of auditory strangulation from the plant name's 'i's and 'ee's.

By contrast, the most obvious difficulty faced by the translator of 'quittenpastete' ('quince jelly', pp. 72-3) – a radiant celebration of domestic detail and delight – is its (almost perfectly) faithful adherence to the Sapphic stanza form.

This is attempted as rarely in German as in English, and anyone who has faced its complex challenges will know why. Modern English Sapphics are rendered in accentual metre, determined by the stress on a syllable rather than its length, as was the case in Ancient Greek, and the three Sapphic lines, followed by the shorter 'Adonic', are built on a precise sequence of trochees and dactyls, with some flexibility permitted on the free fourth syllable, the 'syllaba anceps', and on the final syllable. The task I set myself, then, was to explore the rich potential of this ancient metre, following its drive syllable for syllable, yet seeking to match it with a flow that is natural enough in English to suggest that no word has been inserted primarily for metrical effect.

Thirdly, a recurrent problem for translators arises when the semantic fields of similar words in two languages do not favourably overlap. The poem 'histories: onesilos' (p. 83) is based on Herodotus's account of Onesilos's attempt to usurp his brother's throne and take over the island of Cyprus. After initial success Onesilos was defeated and killed, and his head placed on the city gate of Amathus, where bees built a hive in his skull. One word for 'hive' in German is 'Bienenstaat' (bee-state) and Jan Wagner uses the term to magical effect. A literal translation of the poem's closing lines would be: "he almost had a land when he still lived. / In his head now lives a whole state" – the German 'staat' being assonant with the end-word 'epitaph' of two lines earlier. The lines play on Onesilos's imperialistic opportunism, and on an annual sacrifice held in his memory. The English translation, as the reader will see, seeks recourse to an entirely different lexical field to capture a similar, albeit not identical, effect. My first thought had been to offer 'memory/colony' as a translation of 'epitaph/staat', which at least retained the *idea* of the bee-specific 'staat' of the second term. 'Colony' was faithful to the bees, but weak by contrast with 'staat'. The version I have finally chosen seeks to emphasize the irony of these lines – essential to the success of the final stanza. (And if you say the word *imperium* several times without interruption it can sound as distressing as an angry swarm).

'elegy for knievel' (p. 95), finally, with its absence of Sapphics, rhyme or strict syllabics, reminds us that imagery and the pertinence of colloquial figures of speech can be no less testing to a translator than metrical forms or rhyme. Some readers will remember the American motorcycle stunt performer and 1970s icon Evel Knievel who undertook 75 ramp-jumps, broke 433 bones, and died aged 69. Like Knievel's famous 1975 Wembley jump over 13 buses, Wagner's unexpectedly empathic enactment of Knievel's dangerous endeavours keeps the reader on the edge of his seat. A more inward stanza, pondering the possible misgivings of the daredevil, only adds to the tension. The challenge for the translator is to keep the adrenalin pumping – metrically and lexically, thereby honouring the performance enacted by the poem itself. I was particularly concerned to insure the authenticity of the last five lines, in which the great entertainer, under a "bruised moon", takes the ramp for a kind of high-octane *nunc stans* in the final line – a weirdly transcendent image, fitting of heroic elegy and itself a pinnacle of translation: capturing not so much the lifework itself, as the spirit of its gesture and historical moment.

Iain Galbraith

[1] Wallace Stevens's 'The Man With the Blue Guitar', (Section XII), *Collected Poetry and Prose* (New York: The Library of America, 1997), 137, 140.
[2] 'Chinaman' and 'googly' are cricketing terms. [*OED*, 2nd Ed.: *googly*: a ball which breaks from the off, though bowled with apparent leg-break action. *Chinaman*: a left-handed bowler's off-break to a right-handed batsman.

INTRODUCTION

Born in Hamburg in 1971, Jan Wagner is widely acknowledged as one of the most important German poets of his generation. Since 1995 he has lived in Berlin as a writer, editor and translator of poetry, especially from the Anglo-Saxon tradition (James Tate, Matthew Sweeney, Simon Armitage, Robin Robertson). He has won many prizes; critics prize his precise language, luminous imagery and effortless play with forms. The word 'virtuoso' is attached to him almost universally. But if this description suggests a poet of showy surface, a poet of effect, nothing could be further from the truth. Instead there is a much more involved interplay of surface and depth. And while the poems appear still, even modest, on the surface, they become more enigmatic, more fluid and more complex, the more one reads them.

Immediately striking is Wagner's precise observation of things, animals and landscapes. The poems of the collections sampled here – *Probebohrung im Himmel* (2001), *Guerickes Sperling* (2004), *Achtzehn Pasteten* (2007), *Australien* (2010), and *Regentonnenvariationen* (2014) – seem then to be for the most part 'thing-poems', a kind of poetry that has a particular tradition in Germany and harks back to Rilke. The repertoire is eclectic – from the exotic to the everyday: mushrooms, fennel, a chameleon, a gecko, sheets, a tea-bag, a see-saw. The power comes from the meticulous and sensual detail, which means that the things are also always more than themselves. And while the poems show absolute respect for the particular thing they address, they also simultaneously explore the poetic possibilities ignited beyond or within it. That possibility comes from a moment of surprise: an unusual angle of observation, from the bottom of a well, perhaps; or an intensity that searches to penetrate a thing and unlock its secrets: "listening for the gentle snap within, / hoping for the right combination" ('mushrooms', p. 27).

But if Wagner's poems turn on the fiercely specific, they are anything but parochial. One feels that his poetic eye is ranging through the world like a camera before coming to rest and teasing out the quiddity of the thing, almost by the sheer force of his attention. Thus a garden rain-butt can open a perspective on continents; or Australia just might be found by digging to the other side of the earth. Wagner is sceptical about those types of poetry that set out to treat the 'big themes' head-on, preferring to concentrate on the subject at hand and allowing the rest to arrive by stealth – almost behind the poem's back. So while almost all the poems dwell stubbornly in the physical, they also nudge (almost) mutely towards the metaphysical:

> this is the village, and this the master
> knacker's dwelling, a wisp of smoke
> snaking skyward from the roof.
>
> the empty hides on the walls. a basket
> of pups, their eyes still sutured
> by blindness, taking their first sniff
>
> of the world. ('dobermann', p. 57)

This relationship inevitably becomes a theme of the poems themselves. It is hard, for example, not to see the chameleon of the poem of that name (p. 81) also as an image of the poet – finely balanced between possibilities:

> an astronomer
> gazing simultaneously at the sky
> and the ground, keeping his distance
> from both.

These are not in any way confessional poems, poems of affect either. Instead, as in Wagner's early models, the Expressionists Georg Heym or Georg Trakl, for example, moods crystallise into images independently of an experiencing I. Despite the focus on things and the apparent security of the traditional forms (I will come back to them), the dominant mood is one of unease. Human beings are for the most part impotent, liminal figures ("more fools than heroes", as another poem, not included here, has it):

> at what point do things begin to evade us,
> how soon do we notice we do not count,
> become mere witnesses or extras... ('the catkin', p. 117)

In contrast, nature is animate, potentially overwhelming and fraught with danger. For all that the poems seem at first to be the poetic equivalent of still lifes, one becomes increasingly aware of the restlessness at their heart: the fretful winds; clouds and ghosts passing; trains rumbling in the distance; earth shifting beneath the feet. The logic of this world is unreliable, and leads to an almost constant sense of anxiety that pervades otherwise innocuous scenes: the flickering of the candles during a power cut in Huntsville, Texas, the "maps of gore" on the white aprons at Smithfield market, the "pale hearts" of the fennel exposed to the knife, that "thrashing fin in the dark". Elsewhere, the landscape, here the Karst, seems to be lying in wait ('olm', p. 119):

> where even today,
> one who goes out
> for a smoke on the fissured
> ground at night,
> high above
> the system of caves,
> can easily go missing...

Every so often the threat is realised out of the blue: apples raining down onto a car roof like children's fists, the flash of a blade, a meteorite or in 'the west' (p. 75):

under our shirts ticks
like pearl-headed pins in our skin:
the wilderness taking our measure.

That same threat makes itself felt linguistically too. In 'giersch' (p. 108) the ground elder of the German (one hears also 'gier' – German for voracity or lust) gradually takes possession of the house. In Iain Galbraith's magnificent translation it is bindweed "choking / windows and drain, trumpeting, binding, abiding, / till nothing breathes but bindweed" (p. 109). We hear the vowel sounds gradually thicken and modulate until they stifle the poem, and in German the last three lines finish with the same word, "giersch", signalling its total occupation of our senses and the poem.

This sonnet is not untypical of Wagner's highly self-conscious play with language. He uses many complex traditional forms – sonnet, haiku, villanelle, Sapphic ode, etc. But he repeatedly emphasises that he does not see these as a restrictive corset, but rather a way of breathing and creating linguistic possibilities. Added to this is the use of rhyme, which operates frequently with half-rhymes and assonances, "dirty rhymes", Galbraith calls them. These are not mistakes or technical inadequacies though (and here one might sense lessons learned from Wagner's translation of contemporary English poetry). Rather they work to give a sense of constant potential slippage. This effect is increased by the fact that he abandons the upper case for line beginnings, but also for nouns, where is it traditionally used in German. Wagner explains how he draws on the resulting lexical and semantic instability to push the reader even further off balance. The word 'regen' can, for instance, be read as the noun for "rain", as the verb "sich regen" (to move or be stirred up) and as the plural form of the adjective of "rege" (i.e., brisk, animated). Added to this is the frank relish with which he draws on arcane vocabulary or technical expressions. Taken together these effects work against the apparent stability of the 'things' to make manifest the inaccessibility, the illegibility, of experience: "the kelp's script / is smudged, rewritten, rubbed out" (p. 51). We are, as Rilke put it, "not so reliably at home in the interpreted world".

But it would be wrong to think of Wagner's vision as necessarily bleak. The observant wonder is laced with an engaging scepticism. One of relatively few lyric subjects that appear in this volume surveys the false weather created to lure earthworms out of the lawn and declares "i distrust every drop" (p. 49). And this scepticism is fed by an eye for the heroically absurd: a catkin lodged in a nose, an elegy for Evel Knievel, the poem as a horse (after Michael Donaghy), two boys in quiet concentration digging their way towards the other side of the world: "the horizon / sporting their spade like a flagpole" ('australia', p. 105).

If one starts then by reading Wagner's poems as still lifes of a sort, meditations, distilled 'thing-poems', it is not long before one notices that in fact they are almost all driven by a kind of inner current of change and exchange. This can take the form of the shining transformation of 'quince jelly' (p. 73), for example, or a more gruesome one of a skull to a buzzing *"imperium"* (p. 83). But it can signal also a moving from obscurity towards language: "we are following the rapids and their / raging grammar to the source" (p. 75), "the pears and apples / grew towards their names" (p. 73). And it also offers a hope for our own coming to ourselves through the poem ('self-portrait with a swarm of bees', p. 127):

> how a person's being
> slowly but steadily gains in weight and spread
> to become the stone-still centre of song...

Finally, in one of Wagner's central poems, we see the transformative power of poetry itself. The poem 'guericke's sparrow' (p. 37) treats the Magdeburg scientist Otto von Guericke's experiments on a sparrow in a glass jar in order to prove the existence of a vacuum:

and now
they watch the sparrow start to flutter
like the flame on a spirit of wine – its air
grown ever thinner.

Yet this destructive depletion, echoed in a number of poems, is answered by an exorbitant and energising possibility of metamorphosis: "'that dead sparrow,' whispers one, / 'will one day fly through an empty sky'". That possibility is in turn metamorphosed and brought brilliantly to life in these luminous translations.

Karen Leeder

SELF-PORTRAIT WITH A SWARM OF BEES

CHAMPIGNONS

wir trafen sie im wald auf einer lichtung:
zwei expeditionen durch die dämmerung
die sich stumm betrachteten. zwischen uns nervös
das telegraphensummen des stechmückenschwarms.

meine großmutter war berühmt für ihr rezept
der champignons farcis. sie schloß es in
ihr grab. alles was gut ist, sagte sie,
füllt man mit wenig mehr als mit sich selbst.

später in der küche hielten wir
die pilze ans ohr und drehten an den stielen –
wartend auf das leise knacken im innern,
suchend nach der richtigen kombination.

MUSHROOMS

we came across them in a forest glade:
two expeditions in crepuscular light
mutely eying each other. between us
the telegraphic whine of swarming gnats.

my grandmother was famed for her recipe
for champignons farcis. she locked it away
in her grave. all that is good, she told us,
should be filled with little more than itself.

later in the kitchen we held
the mushrooms to our ears and turned their stems,
listening for the gentle snap within,
hoping for the right combination.

DES TOTEN LENINS REISE NACH TJUMEN

I

der auftrag kam von ganz weit oben, hieß:
das große in die stille retten. hieß:
den radius erweitern. bis tjumen.

II

wir schwitzten bei der arbeit. nicht so sehr
aus sorge ihm zu schaden als aus angst
vor dem was uns erwarten könnte. wenn.

die funzel. unsre schatten in der krypta
wie schmierenpantomimen. ferne schüsse.

III

das dunkel im waggon. das dunkel draußen.
das leise rattern der schienen. dann ein pfiff

von vorne, von der lok, der jubelnd versuchte
sich in den spalt zwischen himmel und erde zu zwängen:

der ural gab uns an die ebene frei.

IV

wir blickten nur selten durch die ritzen im holz:
im trüben licht eines tages gähnte die taiga.

dann und wann ein luchs – bewegungslos
als versuche er, einen namen zu erinnern.

DEAD LENIN'S JOURNEY TO TYUMEN

I

the order came from the very top, said:
take this greatness to peace, to safety. said:
extend the radius. to tyumen.

II

we sweated as we worked. but less from fear
of damaging him than out of a dread
of what might happen to us if we did.

the dim lantern, our shadows in the crypt
like a hammy dumb-show. distant gunfire.

III

the gloom in the carriage. the darkness outside.
the low rattle of the tracks. then a whistle blast

from the fore, from the engine, gleefully trying
to squeeze through the crack between heaven and earth –

and the urals released us to the plains.

IV

we rarely looked through the chinks in the wood –
in bleary daylight the yawning taiga,

now and then a lynx – motionless,
as if trying to remember someone's name.

einen geburtstag? einen abzählreim?

    v

und er, der immer zwischen uns lag – er sah
mit ernst und zuversicht in eine zukunft
die nicht die unsere war: tag um tag

die der sumpf verschluckte als wären es billige pillen
gegen die eigene, ewige schlaflosigkeit.

    vi

das dunkel im waggon. das dunkel draußen.
das leise rattern der schienen.

a birthday? a children's counting rhyme?

    V

and he who had always lain between us looked
with grave assurance into a future
that was not ours: day after day swallowed

by the marshland like cut-price pills
against its own unending insomnia.

    VI

the gloom in the carriage. the darkness outside.
the low rattle of the tracks.

FENCHEL

knollen vor einem gemüseladen im winter –
wie bleiche herzen, sagtest du, gedrängt
in einer kiste, wärme suchend – so daß wir

sie mit uns nahmen und nach hause trugen,
wo feuer im kamin entzündet war,
wo kerzen auf dem tisch entzündet waren,

und ihnen halfen aus ihrer dünnen haut,
die strünke kappten, die zitternden blätter entfernten
und sie zu feinen weißen flocken hackten,

wartend, bis das wasser kochte,
die fensterscheibe blind war vom dampf.

FENNEL

bulbs in front of a grocer's in winter –
like pale hearts, you said, crowding
together in a crate for warmth, so we

took them in, carried them home,
where the fire was lit in the hearth,
where candles were lit on the table,

and helping them out of their thin skins,
trimmed their stalks, removed their shivering leaves,
chopped the flesh into white flakes –

waiting until the water had boiled
and the window was blind with steam.

FRÖSCHE

das zimmer – ein chaos. was noch nicht verkauft ist
formt auf dem boden die schwer zu entziffernde formel

seines bestrebens: drähte, instrumente
und bücher. leere flaschen. seine frau

ist lange fort. und auch der letzte zahn:
»ohne ehrfurcht vorm eigenen körper« wie achim

von arnim meinte, kämpft er mit dem wein
und mit der prämisse: alles leben besteht

aus elektrizität. draußen am see
ist es plötzlich unheimlich still – die frösche geben

einander heimlich das neue codewort durch.

Von 1800 bis zu seinem frühen Tod im Jahre 1810 unternahm der Naturwissenschaftler Johann Wilhelm Ritter – angeregt durch die Entdeckungen Luigi Galvanis – zahlreiche Selbstversuche mit der sogenannten Voltaschen Säule.

FROGS

his room – in chaos. across the floor the things
he hasn't sold construe the barely decipherable

formula of his endeavours: wires, instruments
and books. empty bottles. his wife –

long gone, his last tooth too:
"lacking in respect for his own body", as achim

von arnim opined, he battles with the wine
as with the premise that all of life consists

of electricity. all at once,
down by the lake, an uncanny stillness – the frogs,

on the sly, are passing on the latest codeword.

From 1800 until his early death in 1810 the scientist Johann Wilhelm Ritter – inspired by the discoveries of Luigi Galvani – undertook a series of experiments on himself using the so-called Voltaic pile.

GUERICKES SPERLING

>»...*köstlicher als Gold, bar jeden*
>*Werdens und Vergehens*...«
>   OTTO VON GUERICKE

was ist das, unsichtbar und doch so mächtig,
daß keine kraft ihm widersteht? der kreis
von bürgern rund um meister guericke
und seine konstruktion: die vakuumpumpe,
die auf drei beinen in das zimmer ragt,
vollendet und mit der obszönen grazie
der mantis religiosa. messingglanz,
die kugel glas als rezipient: hier sitzt
der sperling, der wie eine weingeistflamme
zu flackern angefangen hat – die luft,
die immer enger wird. vorm fenster reifen
die mirabellen, summt die wärme, wächst
das gras auf den ruinen. an der wand
ein kupferstich vom alten magdeburg.
die unbeirrbarkeit der pendeluhr,
diopter, pedometer, astrolabium;
der globus auf dem tisch, wo eben erst
neuseelands rückenflosse den pazifik
durchschnitten hat, und wie aus weiter ferne
das zähe trotten eines pferdefuhrwerks.
»dieser tote sperling«, flüstert einer,
»wird noch durch einen leeren himmel fliegen.«

GUERICKE'S SPARROW

> "...*more exquisite than gold, devoid
> of all becoming or passing away...*"
> OTTO VON GUERICKE

for what is hid from sight yet so robust
that naught can counter its power? a group
of burghers girdling master guericke
and his construction: the vacuum pump,
standing on three legs in the room, a perfect
piece whose poise recalls the obscene grace
of the mantis religiosa. polished brass,
its recipient a sphere of glass: and now
they watch the sparrow start to flutter
like the flame on a spirit of wine – its air
grown ever thinner. beyond the window
mirabelles grow ripe in the buzzing heat,
the grass spreads on the ruins. a copperplate
engraving hangs on the wall: old magdeburg.
the pendulum clock's relentless progress;
pedometer, dioptre, astrolabe;
the globe on the table where new zealand's
dorsal lately carved the great pacific,
and then, like a sound arrived from far away,
the obstinate trot of a horse and cart.
"that dead sparrow", whispers one,
"will one day fly through an empty sky."

WEIHNACHTEN IN HUNTSVILLE, TEXAS

»Es ist so, als ob man an einem Bahndamm wohnt.
Zuerst achtet man noch auf jeden Zug, dann hört man
sie einfach nicht mehr.«
       EIN EINWOHNER VON HUNTSVILLE

als der strom an diesem abend
zusammensackte, flackerten die lampen
am weihnachtsbaum, erloschen. in der ferne
der spätzug. wir, die nacht, der bratenduft –
die gänse schwammen friedlich in den seen
aus weißem porzellan. im mondlicht
die abgenagten knochen der veranden.
wir lauschten auf die leicht bewegte wiege
des großen waldes, der die stadt umfängt,
dann kehrten die choräle ins radio zurück.
in jedem fernseher saß ein präsident.
der bahndamm, ohne anfang, ohne ende.
der gänsebraten.

CHRISTMAS IN HUNTSVILLE TEXAS

> "It's like living next to some railroad embankment.
> At first you notice every train, then you just don't
> hear them any more."
> A CITIZEN OF HUNTSVILLE

that evening when the power
failed, the lights on the christmas tree flickered
and died. we heard the late train
from afar. just us, the night, the smell
of roast – the geese floating peacefully
in lakes of milky porcelain. in the moonlight
the gnawed bones of the verandas.
we strained our ears for the gentle sway
of the huge forest that cradled the town,
then the radios filled with carols again.
a president sat in every tv-set.
the railroad, without beginning or end.
the roast goose.

KLEINSTADTELEGIE

die schattenkarawane, jeden morgen
ihr aufbruch, und die waschanlage,
die stets aus einem reinen schlaf erwachte.

und in den lieferwagen pendelten
die schweinehälften zwischen ja und nein,
den linden wuchsen herzen. und es paßte

nicht mehr als ein blatt papier zwischen mich und die welt.
und in den gärten, hinter allen hecken
verkündeten die rasenmäher den mai.

SMALL TOWN ELEGY

the caravan of shadows leaving
every morning, and the car wash
always waking from a spotless sleep.

and in the butchers' vans the sides
of pork that swung between a yes and a no
and lindens grew fresh hearts. and no more

than a sheet of paper came between me and the world.
and in the gardens, behind the hedges,
the lawn mowers ushered in the may.

DER VETERANENGARTEN

> »Again he fighting with his foe, counts o'er his scars,
> Tho' Chelsea's now the seat of all his wars,
> And fondly hanging on the lengthening tale,
> Reslays his thousands o'er a mug of ale.«
> Sir John Soane, Inschrift im Summerhouse
> des Royal Hospital, London

die veteranen wachsen aus dem gras
empor in ihren ehrenuniformen;
die schweren messingknöpfe blinzeln matt
ins späte licht des nachmittags zurück.
sie wachsen aus dem gras wie in den mythen
das heer der ausgesäten drachenzähne.

die veteranen zeigen ihre zähne
auf fotos, die so braun wie altes gras
geworden sind – vergilbter noch als mythen.
der kampf, sagt jener grieche, ist der formen
beginn, und alles führt zu ihm zurück.
die veteranen steigen auf das matt-

erhorn ihrer erinnerung, das matt
im gegenlicht erstrahlt. die falschen zähne,
die längst schon in der ebene zurück-
geblieben sind. fast unbemerkt im gras
die enkel, glücklich mit geringsten formen
des spiels – ein gegensatz zum kaum bemühten

versuch der veteranen, sich beim mythen-
umrankten spiel der könige ins matt
zu setzen. (die die weißen steine formen
benutzen elfenbein und walroßzähne.)
im veteranengarten wächst das gras.
die schnecke gleitet in ihr haus zurück.

THE VETERANS' GARDEN

> "Again he fighting with his foe, counts o'er his scars,
> Tho' Chelsea's now the seat of all his wars,
> And fondly hanging on the lengthening tale,
> Reslays his thousands o'er a mug of ale."
> — SIR JOHN SOANE, INSCRIPTION IN THE SUMMER HOUSE
> AT THE ROYAL HOSPITAL, LONDON

the veterans grow out of the cropped grass,
attired in their honorary uniforms.
their imposing brass buttons, rendered matt
in this late light, no longer twinkle back.
they grow out of the grass, recalling the myths
where an army was sown from the dragon's teeth.

the veterans manage still to bare their teeth
on photographs as brown as withered grass
in summer – in fact more faded than those myths.
of conflict, so the greek sage tells us, all forms
are born – to struggle too all things lead back.
and now the veterans assault their matt-

erhorn of memories, its glow grown matt
against the failing light: such feats, and false teeth,
so easy to forget, often stay back
in the plains. almost unseen in the grass
their grandchildren revel in the simplest forms
of distraction – unlike these veteran smiths

of doom, engrossed in a game of crowns and myths
where king fights king and knights deliver mate.
(traditionally, the artisan who forms
these men uses ivory and walrus teeth.)
in the veterans' garden grows the grass.
the snail that ventured from its house slides back.

die veteranen denken oft zurück
und kaum nach vorne. so entstehen mythen.
die enkelkinder spielen auf dem gras
in das die kameraden bissen, matt
vom kampf. zu leben heißt: man muß die zähne
zusammenbeißen. und das schicksal formen.

die schwestern tragen weiße uniformen
und sind doch warm. sie rollen sie zurück
ins haus wenn erste sterne ihre zähne
entblößen, und ein ganzes heer von mythen
folgt ihnen auf die zimmer. wo es matt
war vom gewicht erhebt sich nun das gras.

die dunklen formen wandern übers gras –
man mag an zähne denken. oder mythen.
der könig bleibt zurück in seinem matt.

the veterans' thoughts often take them back
but rarely forward, and what transpires are myths:
their grandkids playing on the very grass
on which their comrades fell, whose eyes grew matt
in death; fundamental, then, to grit your teeth
and bear it, to master fate in all its forms.

the nurses are out in their white uniforms
and yet they stay so warm. they wheel them back
inside as soon as the first stars flash their teeth,
and as they leave the scene an army of myths
goes with them to their rooms. no longer matt,
its imprints rise and glint in starlit grass.

the dark forms shift across the perfect grass –
something tries to remind us of teeth. or myths.
the king stays behind in his place: checkmate.

SMITHFIELD MARKET

was wir hier suchten, hier verloren glaubten?
wer weiß. erhellt hinter der abgelebten
fassade einer frühen morgenstunde
der alte markt, die halle, ihre stände
mit rohem fleisch beladen: über kisten
und tiefkühltruhen an der decke kreisten
die schwärme blanker haken. lose rippen,
im kilo billiger, in kleinen gruppen
die schlachter – rauchend, zeitung lesend, scherzend.
der plan aus blut auf ihren weißen schürzen
nicht zu entschlüsseln. plötzlich vis-à-vis
der abgetrennte schweinskopf hinter glas.
in seinen zügen auf den zweiten blick
zufriedenheit und so etwas wie glück.

SMITHFIELD MARKET

who knows what we were looking for here,
or what we thought we'd lost. in the glare
behind the tired façade of the early hour
we found the covered market halls, and counters
piled with raw meat: above the crates
and storage freezers swarms of shining hooks
circled under the ceiling. spare ribs
were selling cheaper by the kilo, in small groups
the butchers smoked and read their papers, joked,
the maps of gore on their white coats
not to be deciphered. suddenly, vis-à-vis –
the severed head of a pig behind the glass.
at second glance, searching its face, we see
contentedness, and something else, like bliss.

REGENWÜRMER

in jenem sommer lag die erde rissig
und trocken da. mit wechselstrom und drähten
im boden schufen wir ein falsches wetter,
die würmer anzulocken, jene zwitter
an dünne haken auszuliefern. jahre später

seh ich am himmel ihre schatten ziehen, riesig,
in dunklen wolken, präsentiert sich mir die welt
vorm fenster als kaltes quadrat. ich warte auf das klopfen
an meiner tür und vor der scheibe fällt und fällt
der regen. ich mißtraue jedem tropfen.

EARTHWORMS

that summer the earth lay dry
and cracked before us. using alternating current
and wires in the ground we created a false weather
to lure the worms, hermaphrodites we meant
to thread on hooks. years later

i see their gigantic shadows drifting by
in sombre clouds, while the world beyond the window
looks like a cold square. i wait for the knock
at my door and watch the streams of rain flow
down the glass. i distrust every drop.

KOLUMBUS

kolumbus steht versunken da, die tafel
ist eine leere fläche. grün das segel draußen
des ahorns und der lärm von genua;
ein wind vom hafen her, wo die matrosen
mit scharfem atem von antilia schwafeln,
der aussätzige seine stigmata
wie eine karte ihre weißen male
zur schau stellt, sich die taue an der mole
im schlaf zusammenrollen und die schrift
des tangs verwischt, geschrieben wird, verwischt –
als ob das meer noch lerne, mit kolumbus
gemeinsam, der sich eben jetzt die kopfnuß
vom lehrer einfängt: hart und so bestimmt,
daß der boden unter den füßen zu schwanken beginnt.

COLUMBUS

there stands columbus, lost in thought,
the board an empty space, and in the court
the maple's green sail, the clatter and clamour
of genoa. a breeze blows from the harbour
where the sailors gabble on about antillia,
the abject leper exposes his stigmata
like a mappemonde's white birthmarks,
while hawsers left in heaps out on the mole flex,
coiling in their sleep, and the kelp's script
is smudged, rewritten, rubbed out –
as if the sea were still at school, a classmate
of columbus, who even now receives a clout
about the lugs from his preceptor, so hard
the earth begins to shift beneath his feet.

STÖRTEBEKER

»*Ich bin der neunte, ein schlechter Platz.
Aber noch läuft er.*«
GÜNTER EICH

noch läuft er, sieht der kopf dem körper zu
bei seinem vorwärtstaumel. aber wo
ist er, er selbst? in diesen letzten blicken
vom korb her oder in den blinden schritten?
ich bin der neunte und es ist oktober;
die kälte und das hanfseil schneiden tiefer
ins fleisch. wir knien, aufgereiht, in tupfern
von weiß die wolken über uns, als rupfe
man federvieh dort oben – wie vor festen
die frauen. vater, der mit bleichen fäusten
den stiel umfaßt hielt, und das blanke beil,
das zwinkerte im licht. das huhn derweil
lief blutig, flatternd, seinen weg zu finden
zwischen zwei welten, vorbei an uns johlenden kindern.

STÖRTEBEKER

> *"I am the ninth, a bad position.
> But he's still walking."*
> GÜNTER EICH

he's still walking, his head watching his body
stagger on. but wait, where is he really,
where is his true self? in those last looks
he gave from the basket, or these blind steps?
i am the ninth and the month is october;
the cold and hempen rope cut deeper
into the flesh. we kneel in a row, high
above us dabs of downy white in the sky –
like when the women, on the eve of some feast,
would pluck the fowls. then father's ashen fist
clenched the haft of the axe, its burnished blade
flashed in the sun, and the hen, a mess of blood
and fluttering feathers, made its eyeless tracks
between two worlds, past us jeering brats.

DER MANN AUS DEM MEER

man findet ihn in einem frack aus salz
und sand. ein paß aus algen, ein ensemble
von heringsmöwen hinter ihm. der nebel.

er spricht nicht, dafür läßt er am klavier die filz-
brandung hüpfen, durchs gehäuse wogen,
daß man erstaunt. die schweren epauletten
der hände, die sich auf die schultern legen;
die stunde ruhm, die ära der tabletten,

die nächte im herbst: auf den gängen treiben die pfleger
wie eisberge vorüber. in dem klinik-
garten unter den mauern ein geflacker
letzter blätter, aus dem alten schuppen,
an dem der efeu steigt, gedämpftes klingen
eines klaviers. man hält es für chopin.

THE MAN FROM THE SEA

they find him in a dinner suit of salt
and sand, his passport seaweed, an ensemble
of herring gulls behind him in the drizzle.

he says nothing, but lets the surging felt-
surf caper through the piano case
to grand surprise. the heavy epaulettes
of hands weigh on his shoulders: this
is his hour of fame, a time of tablets,

autumn nights with nurses floating
like icebergs through the wards. in the clinic
garden the last leaves flutter
beneath the walls. from an old cabin,
where ivy rises, drifts the muted tinkle
of a piano. some believe it is chopin.

DOBERMANN

für Ron Winkler

dies ist das dorf, und dies am waldesrand
die wasenmeisterei, von deren dach
ein dünner rauch sich in den himmel stiehlt.

die leeren felle an der wand. der korb
mit welpen, ihre augen noch vernäht
von blindheit: so beschnüffeln sie die welt.

noch ist es früh, und in den städten schlafen
die landvermesser und die kartographen.
im garten jener brunnen voller durst.

apolda, thüringen: die tote kuh
am feldrand, ein gestrandeter ballon,
von seuche aufgebläht. sie wird

dort liegenbleiben: unter einem kleingeld
von sternen schreitet er, an dessen seite
zwei schwarze klingen durch die landschaft schneiden.

DOBERMANN

for Ron Winkler

this is the village, and this the master
knacker's dwelling, a wisp of smoke
snaking skyward from the roof.

the empty hides on the walls. a basket
of pups, their eyes still sutured
by blindness, taking their first sniff

of the world. it is early, cartographers and land
surveyors in the towns are still abed.
that well in the garden brims with thirst.

apolda, thuringia: the dead cow
at the edge of the field is a grounded balloon,
bloated with plague. it will lie there

a while yet. he strides out under the small
coin of the stars. and at his side
the two black blades keep slicing through the fields.

QUALLEN

>*»The very deep did rot: O Christ!*
>*That ever this should be!«*
>   Samuel Coleridge, *The Rime of the Ancient Mariner*

sie waren immer da. an jenem morgen
jedoch schien sich das wasser zu verhärten
ums boot herum. das ruder stak im meer
wie in zu dickem eintopf, und wir männer
erschraken. abends war der strand,
die promenade voll von fremden leuten.

wie kleine glocken, nur daß man ihr läuten
nicht wahrnahm, rief am nächsten morgen
der mann, der sich ein holzpodest am strand
errichtet hatte. noch im halbschlaf hörten
wir, wie er in den küstenwind um manna
zu flehen schien. das zähe, bleiche meer.

drei tage, und es wurden immer mehr.
als gäbe es bis zu den aleuten
nur unser dorf, sonst keines: muskelmänner
und primadonnen, buden, »magic morgan
und sein panoptikum«. und ganze herden
von trunkenen, die sich vom ost- zum westrand

der bucht ergingen. erst als selbst der strand
bedeckt war von gallerte, sich das meer
hinanschob, gingen sie, und die behörden
umzäunten das gelände. von den leuten
sprach niemand mehr von omen, von dem morgen
des jüngsten tages, von klabautermännern.

JELLYFISH

> "*The very deep did rot: O Christ!*
> *That ever this should be!*"
> SAMUEL COLERIDGE, *The Rime of the Ancient Mariner*

there were always some. but that morning
the water seemed thicker, almost hard
around the boat. stuck in the sea
the rudder choked, and we men
were sore afraid. that evening the beach
and front were crowded with strange people.

"like little bells", except that people
wouldn't hear, cried the man the next morning
who'd built himself a pulpit on the beach.
still half-asleep in bed we heard
him rail at the wind, intone amen
as if on bended knee to that unyielding sea.

as if between this beach and the bering sea
ours was the only village, more people
poured in every day: muscle-men
and prima donnas, stalls, "mister morning
and his noted cup of tea", a horde
of staggering drunks across the beach

from east to west. only when the beach
too became a mass of jelly and the sea
had merged with the land did that herd
leave, the constable raise a fence. people
no longer spoke of spirits, the morning
come of judgement day, or foulest omen.

wann wird die ausnahme zur regel? männer
mit fahne, unrasierte ministrant-
en, löcher in den kleidern. ob es morgen,
ob abend war – es scherte keinen mehr.
zur mittagsstunde dreizehnfaches läuten.
und kinder, die zu niemandem gehörten.

erst schenkte man dem jungen kein gehör, denn
es schien kaum glaublich. bis es uns zwei männer
bestätigten. bald hatten alle etwas läuten
hören, strömten zusammen: hinterm strand,
als wäre nichts geschehen, lag das meer,
der lauf der wellen. – morgen, übermorgen

die frauen an den herden, die am morgen
schon mit den töpfen läuten, und am strand
wir männer, schweigend, mit dem blick aufs meer.

when do exceptions become the rule? men
reeking of drink, unshaven priests, botch-
work, holes in clothes: whether morning
or evening, nobody cared. did we see
our children's forlorn faces? were the people
blind? it chimed thirteen, and nobody heard.

when the boy piped up not one of us heard –
for how could it be true? then two men
confirmed the news. soon all our people
flocked together to look: beyond the beach,
as if nothing had happened, lay the sea –
the incoming waves. the very next morning

women returned to the hearth, all morning
people banging pots and pans, while on the beach
we men stood in silence, gazing out to sea.

DECEMBER 1914

> »*One of the nuts belonging to the regiment got out of the trenches and started to walk towards the German lines.*«

natürlich dachten wir, daß sie plemplem
geworden waren, als sie ungeschützt
aus ihrer deckung traten, nur mit plum-
pudding und mistelzweig – doch kein geschütz

schlug an. wir trafen sie im niemandsland,
unschlüssig, was zu tun sei, zwischen gräben
und grenzen, schlamm und draht, und jede hand
an ihrer hosennaht. bis wir die gaben

verteilten: einer hatte zigaretten
dabei und einer bitterschokolade,
ein dritter wußte mittel gegen ratten
und läuse. die an diesem punkt noch lade-

hemmung hatten, zückten nach dem rum
familienfotos, spielten halma
und standen lärmend, wechselten reihum
adressen, uniformen, helme,

bis kaum etwas im schein der leuchtspurgarben
auf diesem aufgeweichten, nackten anger
zu tauschen übrig blieb außer den gräben
im rücken, ihrem namenlosen hunger.

DECEMBER 1914

> *"One of the nuts belonging to the regiment got out of the trenches and started to walk towards the German lines."*

'course we thought they'd gone loco,
each man-jack a sitting duck
armed with nothing but mistletoe
and plum-pud. but they were in luck –

the guns were still. in no-man's-land
and mud we met between the lines,
at a loss for words, each hand
at a trouser seam, until the woodbines

did the rounds, were lit, and someone
shared a bar of bitter chocolate.
one man had news of a poison
that did away with louse and rat,

others, still too stiff to talk, swigged
rum, or got out family photos,
played halma, yelled, swapped
addresses, uniforms, helmets, jocose

till under the sheaves of streaking tracer
on that soft and naked common field
there was nothing left to offer
but the trenches and their nameless yield.

ANOMALIEN

woher der zettel kam – nicht auszumachen,
von nichts gewußt zu haben ehrensache,
doch unleugbar die neuigkeit: herr richter
besaß drei brustwarzen. das dünne kichern
der mädchen hinter uns – als würden steck-
nadeln herunterfallen. vor dem fenster
vorweihnachtlicher schnee, ein zug weit weg,
der kurz das felderweiß vom weiß darüber trennte,
als wir beim klingelton zusammenzuckten:
im flur auf endlosen regalen hockten
in ihren himmeln aus formaldehyd
die nackten kleinen götter, sahen stumm
uns nach. als ahnten sie, was tief unter der haut
verborgen lag, heranwuchs, und warum.

ANOMALIES

impossible to trace the note back to its author,
for keeping mum was thought a point of honour,
and yet the news was plain – herr richter
had three nipples. a tinkling peel of laughter
passed along the row of girls behind us
and died like showering pins. beyond the window:
early christmas snow. a distant train was
splitting the white sky from the white below
when the bell brought us up with a jolt:
in the corridor on endless shelves, afloat
in their heavens of formaldehyde,
were tiny naked gods – each dewy eye
observed us pass. as if they had identified
what lowered beneath our skin, and why.

SHEPHERD'S PIE

schafe sind wolken, die den boden lieben.
der schäfer liebt marie. streut nüsse auf
den hang, souffliert die drei berühmten worte.
die herde blökt, frißt sie als weiße schrift
aufs tafelgrün. dahinter springt der punkt,
der hirtenhund. am grund des tales zieht
man abendschatten vor die fenster. sieht
den hang nicht und die hügel, nicht die wolken.
wolken, die schafe sind, vom wind getrieben.

SHEPHERD'S PIE

sheep are clouds who love the ground.
the shepherd's in love with marie. he scatters
nuts on the slope, elicits the three famous words.
the flock bleats, gobbling them up as white script
on a green board. behind them bounces dot,
the sheepdog. in windows down in the valley
they are drawing the evening shadows. they
do not see the slope or hillside, nor the clouds:
clouds that are sheep the wind has found.

PÂTÉ CHAUD DE HARENGS AUX POMMES DE TERRE

als joost, der fischer, sich links an die brust griff
und torkelte, verstanden wir: das herz.
als junger mann sei er auf einem frachtschiff
zur see gefahren – veritabler schürz-

enjäger, trinker –, hieß es, und das meer
sei blau und weit der wind. doch er blieb stumm.
selbst wenn nicht wasser in den gläsern war,
das rote auge seiner pfeife glomm;

und glaubte man, daß er sich zu erwärmen
begönne, etwas ihm im mundwinkel
zu zucken schien, sprach er bloß von den schwärmen
tief unten. jenem flossenschlag im dunkel.

PÂTÉ CHAUD DE HARENGS AUX POMMES DE TERRE

when, clutching at his left breast, joost the fisher
staggered, we all knew what was wrong: his heart.
he had gone to sea, they said, on a freighter
as a young man – a renowned chaser of skirt,

so the story went, a drinker, and the sea
ran blue, wind blew where it listed. but he stayed
mum, even when the cups weren't filled with tea,
the banter easy, and his pipe's red eye glowed.

and just when you'd start to think he was warming,
and a flicker of something appeared to lurk
on his lips, he spoke only of the swarming
shoals deep down. that thrashing fin in the dark.

CHEESE AND ONION PASTIES

»Mein Herz ist aus Stein, sagen die Männer,
aber was wissen die von Steinen.«
　　　　　　　　　MARIA BARNAS

was ich von steinen weiß, ist ihr gewicht
im bauch von wölfen, und im bauch von brunnen
das echo nach dem fall; wie ich sie grübeln
zu sehen meinte, nachts im mai einmal
an einem berghang, mondbeschienen, fahl
wie zwiebeln. aber was weiß ich von zwiebeln,
bis auf ihr kleid aus schalen und das brennen,
ihr herz, das sich zurückzieht, schicht um schicht.

CHEESE AND ONION PASTIES

"I have a heart of stone, men say,
but what do they know about stones."
                                    MARIA BARNAS

what i know about stones is their weight
in the bellies of wolves; and that on falling
into the belly of a well they echo;
or how they seemed to ponder, one may night
on the side of a hill, bathed in moonlight,
and as pale as onions. what though do i know
of onions but their frocks, the way they sting,
and layer by layer their retiring heart.

QUITTENPASTETE

wenn sie der oktober ins astwerk hängte,
ausgebeulte lampions, war es zeit: wir
pflückten quitten, wuchteten körbeweise
   gelb in die küche

unters wasser. apfel und birne reiften
ihrem namen zu, einer schlichten süße –
anders als die quitte an ihrem baum im
   hintersten winkel

meines alphabets, im latein des gartens,
hart und fremd in ihrem arom. wir schnitten,
viertelten, entkernten das fleisch (vier große
   hände, zwei kleine),

schemenhaft im dampf des entsafters, gaben
zucker, hitze, mühe zu etwas, das sich
roh dem mund versagte. wer konnte, wollte
   quitten begreifen,

ihr gelee, in bauchigen gläsern für die
dunklen tage in den regalen aufge-
reiht, in einem keller von tagen, wo sie
   leuchteten, leuchten.

QUINCE JELLY

when october hung them among the leaves, those
bulging lanterns, then it was time: we picked ripe
quinces, lugged the baskets of yellow bounty
    into the kitchen,

soused the fruits in water. the pears and apples
grew towards their names, to a simple sweetness –
unlike quinces, clinging to branches in some
    shadowy border's

alphabet, obscure in our garden's latin,
tough and foreign in their aroma. we cut,
quartered, cored the flesh (we were four adult hands,
    two somewhat smaller),

veiled by clouds of steam from the blender, poured in
sugar, heat and effort to something that – raw –
made our palates baulk. but then who could, who would
    hope to explain them:

quinces, jellied, lined up in bellied jars on
shelves and set aside for the darkness, stored for
harsher days, a cellar of days, in which they
    shone, are still shining.

DER WESTEN

der fluß denkt in fischen. was war es also,
das sergeant henley ihm als erster
entriß, die augen gelb und starr, die barteln
zwei schürhaken ums aschengraue maul,
das selbst die hunde winseln ließ?

die stromschnellen und ihre tobende
grammatik, der wir richtung quelle folgen.
die dunstgebirge in der ferne,
die ebenen aus gras und ab und zu
ein eingeborener, der amüsiert
zu uns herüberschaut und dann
im wald verschwindet: all das tragen wir
in adams alte karte ein, benennen
arten und taten. fieber in den muskeln
und über wochen die diät aus wurzeln
und gottvertrauen. unterm hemd die zecken
wie abstecknadeln auf der haut: so nimmt
die wildnis maß an uns.

seltsames gefühl: die grenze
zu sein, der punkt, an dem es endet und
beginnt. am feuer nachts kreist unser blut
in wolken von moskitos über uns,
während wir mit harten gräten
die felle aneinandernähen, schuhe
für unser ziel und decken für die träume.
voraus das unberührte, hinter uns
die schwärmenden siedler, ihre charta
aus zäunen und gattern; hinter uns
die planwagen der händler,
die großen städte, voller lärm und zukunft.

THE WEST

the river thinks in fish. what was it then
that sergeant henley was the first to wrest
from its grasp, its eyes staring yellow, its barbels
two poker hooks around an ash-grey mouth
that made even our dogs whimper?

we are following the rapids and their
raging grammar to the source.
the distant haze of mountains,
grassy plains, and now and then
a native throwing an amused look
in our direction only to vanish
in the forest: all this we enter
on adam's ancient chart, naming
species and deeds. fever in our muscles
and week for week a diet of roots
and trust in god. under our shirts ticks
like pearl-headed pins in our skin:
the wilderness taking our measure.

strange feeling being
the frontier, the point of ending
and beginning. at night by the fire our blood
circles above us in clouds of mosquitoes
while we sew the hides together
with hard fish-bones: shoes
for our destination, blankets for our dreams.
before us untouched land, behind us
the raving settlers, their charta
of fences and gates, behind us
the covered wagons of traders,
gigantic cities, full of noise and future.

STANISZÓW

wo wir unter obstbäumen hielten.
wo mit grünen eidechsenfüßen
der efeu die wände des schlosses hinauflief,
die alten in ihre fischteiche starrten
wie in fotoalben. die fallenden
blätter im park. eine bachforelle
wagte den sprung ins nächste kapitel.

wo abends hinterm weißen mond
eines lampenschirms die falter kreisten,
schnurrend mit ihrer flügelmechanik,
die panischen ziffern einer uhr.
tage im langsamen monat august
und ein letztes aufschäumen in den beeten.
später auf dem autodach das trommeln
der äpfel, hart und klein wie kinderfäuste.

STANISZÓW

where we stayed under fruit trees.
where with green lizards' claws
the ivy scaled the walls of the palace,
the aged stared into their fishponds
as if into photo albums. the leaves
falling in the park. a brown trout
making a leap for the next chapter.

where all evening behind the white
moon of a lampshade circling moths
purred through the workings of their wings –
the panicked numbers of a clock.
days in the slow month of august
and a final frothing of flowerbeds.
later, drumming on the roof of the car,
apples, small and hard, like children's fists.

TEEBEUTEL

I

nur in sackleinen
gehüllt. kleiner eremit
in seiner höhle.

II

nichts als ein faden
führt nach oben. wir geben
ihm fünf minuten.

TEA-BAG

I

draped only in a
sackcloth mantle. the little
hermit in his cave.

II

a single thread leads
to the upper world. we shall
give him five minutes.

CHAMÄLEON

älter als der bischofsstab,
den es hinter sich herzieht, die krümme
des schwanzes. komm herunter, rufen wir
ihm zu auf seinem ast, während die zunge
als teleskop herausschnellt, es das sternbild
einer libelle frißt: ein astronom
mit einem blick am himmel und dem andern
am boden – so wahrt es den abstand
zu beiden. die augenkuppeln, mit schuppen
gepanzert, eine festung, hinter der
nur die pupille sich bewegt, ein nervöses
flackern hinter der schießscharte (manchmal
findet man seine haut wie einen leeren
stützpunkt, eine längst geräumte these).
komm herunter, rufen wir. doch es regt
sich nicht, verschwindet langsam zwischen
den farben. es versteckt sich in der welt.

CHAMELEON

older than the pastoral staff
it drags along behind it, its crook
of a tail. come down, we call
to it on its branch, while its telescope
tongue snaps out to consume
a dragonfly constellation: an astronomer
gazing simultaneously at the sky
and the ground, keeping his distance
from both. the dome of its eye, armour-
plated with scales, is a fortress. only
a pupil moves within, an edgy
flicker behind the arrow-slit (sometimes
you'll find its skin, like some deserted
outpost or long-discarded theory).
come down, we call. but it doesn't
budge, vanishing slowly among
the colours. hiding itself in the world.

HISTORIEN: ONESILOS

(Herodot V, 114)

da oben, der schädel am stadttor,
der mit dem ersten licht zu summen beginnt,
mit dem noch immer leicht verdatter-
ten ausdruck, wo sich ein gesicht befand.

dahinter arbeitet es: die feine
schwarmmechanik im kranium,
die goldenen zahnräder der bienen,
die ineinandergreifen. geranien

und tulpen, wilder mohn und gladiolen –
stück für stück kehrt alles in den blinden
korb zurück, bis in den höhlen
die bienenaugen zu rollen beginnen.

den jungen ist es egal,
wie man ihn nannte, bettler oder könig,
sobald sie über sonnenwarme ziegel
nach oben klettern, der honig,

den er sich ausdenkt, an den händen klebt.
der bienentanz, ein epitaph.
er hatte fast ein land, als er noch lebte.
nun lebt in seinem kopf ein ganzer staat.

HISTORIES: ONESILOS

(Herodotus V, 114)

there, see the skull on the city gate –
it starts to buzz at sunrise
and still wears a vaguely dismayed
grin on what was once a face.

behind it, labour: the swarm's filigree
mechanics in the cranium,
the golden cogwheels of the bees
intermeshed. geranium

and tulip, gladiolus and wild poppy –
everything returns, grain by grain,
to the blind beehive until, in its sockets,
the bees' eyes begin to spin.

it's all the same to the young
what once they called him, king or beggar –
all they want is to climb
the sun-warmed tiles, the nectar

he imagines sticky on their hands.
the dance of the bees, his memoriam.
alive, he almost owned a land –
now, in his head, a whole imperium.

GECKO

sitzt plötzlich dort, als das licht angeht, eilt über die wand: ein wandernder riß, der sich hinten schließt, während er in laufrichtung das weiß zerteilt, rot und pulsierend, eine winzige lavaspalte. was man im schatten des ätna erzählt: daß er nur die wohnungen solcher menschen aufsucht, die freundlichen geistes sind. die dächer von syrakus, die wellen vor messina. tage später sein heller bauch auf dem kiesweg – und binnen stunden ein brodeln von ameisen, das seine form perfekt imitiert, eine wimmelnde mimikry. kieloben liegt das sizilianische fischerboot am strand, ein wrack, seine rippen porös und ausgebleicht von der sonne. am morgen darauf nichts als das zierliche rückgrat, ein verschwindend weißes stäbchen, das übrigbleibt; ein bloßer zahnstocher im breiten maul des august.

GECKO

caught napping when the light flicks on, off it goes scurrying across the wall: a shifting fissure closing up behind itself, its momentum splitting the whiteness as it runs, red and throbbing, a tiny gash of lava. here is what they say about it in the shadow of etna: that it only inhabits the houses of people who have a gentle spirit. the rooftops of syracuse, the waves off messina. days later its pale belly against the gravel path – within hours seething ants are perfectly imitating its shape, a teeming mimicry. the sicilian fishing-boat lies bottom up on the beach, a wreck, with its ribbing already turned porous and bleached by the sun. on the following morning there is nothing left of it but its delicate spine, a white twig that soon will have vanished: a mere toothpick in the gaping maw of august.

VON DEN ÖLBÄUMEN

für Jean-Yves, Robert und Uwe

unter den kronen,
in ihrem schutz gehe ich,
älter als nestor.

*

wie sie sich stemmen
gegen den wind, die brandung
aus blühendem klee.

*

als zögen sie sich
an den eigenen wipfeln
aus dem erdboden.

*

die schneeverwehung
einer schafherde plötzlich
hinter der biegung.

*

leichte süderde,
tiefe wurzeln. der gesang
einer husqvarna.

*

CONCERNING THE OLIVE TREES

for Jean-Yves, Robert and Uwe

amidst the crowns, i
go under their protection,
older than nestor.

*

the way they stand firm
against the wind, the billows
of clover blossom.

*

appearing to pull
themselves out of the earth by
their own top branches.

*

suddenly in front
as we come around the bend,
a snowdrift of sheep.

*

light earth of the south,
deep spread of the roots. the song
of a husqvarna.

*

ein zug schleppt leuchtend
seine fenster vorüber,
gläser voller öl.

*

sagt: welcher prophet
verlor die sandale dort,
aus der schon moos wächst?

*

weißes klebeband
als nachricht in den zweigen:
brailleschrift aus fliegen.

*

stämme, geflochten
wie taue, zwischen himmel
und der unterwelt.

*

ein schwarzer regen
im herbst. darunter parkt der
weiße isuzu.

*

a train passes by,
its lit windows hauled along,
a row of oil jars.

*

tell me: which prophet
lost that sandal, the one that
is sprouting new moss.

*

white sticky tape as
news-tickers in the branches,
in fly-scripted braille.

*

these trunks, braided like
hawsers, joining the heavens
and the underworld.

*

a black rain falling
in autumn. parked under it
the white isuzu.

*

im licht des mondes
sind die stämme noch grauer,
die risse tiefer - - -

*

- - - die alte herde
von elefanten zieht stumm
an mir vorüber.

*

welches gedächtnis
ist da? woran erinnern
sie all die knoten?

*

neben der wurzel
die staubige bierflasche
der marke mythos.

*

der zug. dann sind die
grillen wieder allein in
ihrem heiligtum.

bathed in the moonlight
the trunks are even greyer,
their fissures deeper - - -

*

- - - see, the old herd of
elephants pass in silence
in front of my eyes.

*

what mnemonics is
this? what do so many knots
help you remember?

*

close to the roots a
dusty beer-bottle sporting
the brand name mythos.

*

the train. after which
the crickets are alone in
their sanctuary.

AMISCH

was wir für eine schwarze kutsche hielten,
war nur der schatten einer wolke, saß
als schwarm von raben über einem aas,
bis wir die schwarze kutsche überholten.

die scheunen zwischen tag und nacht, die farmen,
von wäsche blind; das rübenstecken,
das sticken, und wie riesige insekten-
eier die wassertürme in der ferne.

der laden führte bottiche, propan-
gaslampen, einen fahnensaal von sensen.
amanda kaufte eine dieser puppen

ohne gesicht, als prompt zwei pferdebremsen
sich niederließen, ein paar dunkle augen,
die schielten, krabbelten, dann weiterflogen.

AMISH

what we had taken to be a black buggy
was only the shadow of a cloud and fast
became a murder of crows on a carcass,
until we overtook the black buggy.

barns in the daytime, barns by night, their farms
blind with hung laundry; planting turnip,
embroidery, and, like the eggs of gigantic
insects, water towers in the distance.

the store stocked tubs, kerosene tillies,
a whole banner hall of scythes.
amanda bought one of those dolls

without a face, just as two horse flies
settled upon it, a pair of dark eyes
that squinted, crawled, and then flew on.

ELEGIE FÜR KNIEVEL

»God, take care of me – here I come…«

die landschaft zog schlieren, sobald sie ihn sah.
ein draufgänger, ein teufelskerl
mit einem hemd voller sterne
und stets verfolgt von dem hornissenschwarm
des motorenlärms. die knochen brachen,
die knochen wuchsen zusammen, und er sprang.

wie viele hindernisse zwischen rampe
und jenem fernen punkt?
wie viele ausrangierte doppeldecker?
was war ihm der zweifel, der sich eingräbt
im innern, bis ein ganzer cañon klafft
mit rieselndem sand an den rändern,
den schreien großer vögel?

nachmittage, an denen sich die geschichte
für einen augenblick niederließ,
um nach popcorn und abgas zu duften.
wie hier, in yakima, washington,
mit diesem zerbeulten mond überm stadion
und tausenden, denen der atem stockt:
fünfzehn, zwanzig busse und das rad
steht in der luft.

ELEGY FOR KNIEVEL

"God, take care of me – here I come…"

the landscape blurred as soon as it saw him.
a dare-devil, a son of a gun
with his star-spangled shirt
and a bike-engine's swarm of angry hornets
constantly in pursuit. his bones broke,
his bones fixed – and he jumped.

how many obstacles between the ramp
and that distant point?
how many decommissioned double deckers?
did he feel those misgivings cutting
into his innermost self until a whole canyon gaped,
with sand trickling away at the edges
and the screams of giant birds?

on such afternoons history
might take pause for a moment,
sweet with exhaust fumes and popcorn.
like this one in yakima, washington,
with a bruised moon slung over the stadium
and thousands holding their breath:
fifteen, twenty buses, and the wheel
standing still in mid-air.

DER WASSERMANN

für Robin Robertson

einer zog mich mit dem ersten fang
vor husum an bord, den obolus
einer muschel in der heilbuttkalten hand,
um mich herum der silberne applaus

der heringe auf dem deck. ihr heißer grog
verbrannte mich bis auf die gräten,
an anderes gewöhnte ich mich: die glock-
en jeden sonntag. schnee. an federbetten.

man fand den eifersüchtigen bauerntrampel
ertrunken in einer pfütze. eine saat
ging auf. als eines morgens der vergammel-
te dorsch vor meiner tür lag, war es zeit.

ich hinterließ die angst der schlafenden
vorm wasser, eine fußspur, die die sonne
bald auflecken würde, und die gaffenden
nachbarn um mütter und wiegen, ihre söhne

mit fischlippen und schwimmhaut. ohne eile
sank ich zurück zu dem mit flunderaugen ausgelegten
palast, wo meine frau mit ihrer mühle
das salz ins meer dreht. ich wurde meine legende.

THE MERMAN

for Robin Robertson

i was hauled on board by a man
in the first net lifted off husum. the clam
i clutched in my halibut-cold hand
was a fairing, the deck ran agleam

with the silvery applause of the herrings.
the scalding grog seared my gills,
but i soon got used to other things:
snow, their feather beds, and sunday bells.

they discovered that jealous clod
drowned in a puddle. the seed took.
when, one morning, a rotting cod
lay at my door, my hour had struck.

behind me i left their dream-born fears
of water, a trail of footprints the sun
would soon lick dry, gawking neighbours
around the cradles, mothers whose sons

grew fish-lips and web. i was in no hurry,
but to my flounder-eyed palace returned,
where my wife turns out the salt for the sea
from her grinder. i became my own legend.

STEINWAY

der schwarze flügel, den die männer
über die straße hievten,
war der vereiste see aus meiner
kindheit, wo ich kniete,

um durch die blanke fläche
hinabzustarren,
wo zwischen algen und kristall die hechte
für einen augenblick verharrten,

in ihrem dunkel hingen,
jeder eine schimmernde fermate
in einer bis zum knochen dringen-
den urmusik, in ihrer mathe-

matischen, tödlich präzisen
schönheit, für die sekunde,
die wächst, bis sie so groß zu sein
scheint, daß man in ihr siedeln könnte,

weit weg vom weg, vom stein
darauf,
und fast schon festgefroren mit der stirn,
als der puck mich traf.

STEINWAY

the black grand the men
were hauling across the street
was my childhood's frozen
lake; here i knelt

to peer down
through the shiny surface
to where the pike, between
crystal and weed, would briefly poise,

each in its own obscurity
a shimmering fermata
in some primordial harmony,
which, in its mathe-

matical rigor and deadly beauty,
had penetrated to the bone
in a moment that grew and presently
seemed large enough to make a home,

far from the way, far from the stein
or from the way my forehead, stuck
on the ice, felt almost frozen
to it when it was struck by the puck.

WIPPE

mach dich schwerer, rufen sie, also schließe
ich beide augen, denke
an säcke voll zement und eisengieße-
reien, elefanten, an den anker

in seinem schlamm, wo ein manöver wale
vorübergleitet, an das bullenhaupt
eines ambosses. nur eine weile
die luft anhalten, warten. doch nichts hebt

sich oder senkt sich, während ein fasan
schreit und die blätter fallen – meine unwilligen
beine zu kurz, um je den grund zu fassen,
mein kopf beinahe in den wolken.

SEE-SAW

make yourself heavier, they call. i close
both eyes, thinking
of sacks of cement, iron foundries
and elephants, an anchor sinking

in deep mud while a fleet of whales
manoeuvres above it, an anvil's
bullish head. for a while
i hold my breath and wait. to no avail:

nothing goes up, nothing goes down –
a pheasant screams, leaves fall – my legs,
too short, will never reach the ground,
my head is well-nigh in the clouds.

METEORIT

zum beispiel in deinem garten,
zwischen den stock-
tomaten und karotten,
während das kaffeewasser kocht

und du an jenen bauern denkst, der nachts
hinauslief, weil er diebe hörte,
durchs loch im scheunendach
ins rund der älteren taschenlampe starrte,

den küster, der anstelle
von osterglocken
ein stückchen schwärze fand, ein vor die schwelle
gelegtes fündel mit dem glucksen

des jungen himmels tief im innern, an das vieh,
das in der frühe schreit,
die milch, die sauer wird, den mann, der das café
verläßt und einen haufen schrott

entdeckt, in den sein autoschlüssel paßt,
und daran, daß es immer der beginn
eines neuen kultes war, der pest
zum wenigsten, an einem montagmorgen,

an dem der hund des nachbarn plötzlich bellt,
und du zur tür
gehst, etwas älter, doch nicht alt,
und nirgendwo anders als hier.

METEORITE

in your garden, perhaps,
between the tomato vines
and the carrots, just as
you're getting the coffee on

and recalling the farmer who ran
outside, hearing a burglar,
to stare out through a hole in the roof of his barn
into the round of an older

flashlight, the verger who instead
of daffodils
discovered a lump of black, a foundling left
on the threshold, the chuckle

of youthful heavens deep inside it,
cattle lowing in pain in the dawn,
the milk gone sour, a man coming out
of a café to find a ton

of scrap-metal his car-key still fits –
or that it was always the beginning
of some cult, or the moment the plague sets
in, on a monday morning

when the neighbour's dog
suddenly starts to bark and you go to the door
somewhat older, albeit not
old, and no place else but here.

AUSTRALIEN

wir fingen mittags an:
wo sich die brücke in der brache
verlor, von fern die autobahn;
durch ein kaleidoskop zerbroche-

ner flaschen,
ein wurzelwerk von quecken
und alten teppichen; versteckt
hinter dem flüßchen,

dem abwasserrohr mit seinem biblischen
dunkel und dem schlichten
rinnsal, das es predigte.
wir gruben. hinter weißdornbüschen,

der kolonie von schilf, das paläon-
tologische autowrack, wie ein fossil
vom lehm verschluckt. ein fessel-
ballon

mit seiner werbung für bier
oder gelee
zog kühn jenseits der siedlung vorüber,
und ringsherum die glänzend schwarzen egel

entsorgter reifen, vollgesogen
mit schlamm und regenwasser,
die farbkanister, zerschlagen
und liegengelassen.

AUSTRALIA

we started at midday
where the bridge petered
into wasteland and the distant motorway.
through a kaleidoscope of shattered

glass,
old carpets, a tangled
root-mass of couch grass,
hidden behind a runnel,

the sewage pipe with its biblical
murk and the modest trickle
of its sermon:
we dug. behind hawthorn,

a reed-colony, the paleon-
tological wreck of an automobile,
swallowed by loam like a fossil.
a tethered balloon

with its beer or jelly
advert
brashly swung beyond the housing estate
and all around us were the shiny

black leeches of jettisoned tyres, bloated
with mud and rainwater,
the paint cans, battered
and left for litter.

wir gruben; eine grille
verstummte und ein amselpärchen
hüpfte nervös um einen rostigen rechen,
die größere vogelkralle.

wie lange, bis wir es mit felsen
zu tun bekommen würden, kohle-
flözen
und erz? wie lange noch, bis irgendwo ein koala

die erde sich bewegen spürte,
um etwas seltsames zu sehen:
ein loch im boden, zwei verschmierte
jungen, die bis zehn

zu zählen versuchten, dann
verschwanden in dem mythischen, dem most-
richgelben abend, wo am rand
ein spaten steckte wie ein fahnenmast.

we dug. a cricket fell silent
while a pair of blackbirds, panicked,
hopped nervously round a rusty rake,
a larger talon.

how long before we came
up against rock, coal
seams
and ore? how long before a koala

felt the earth shaking
and witnessed something odd? –
a hole in the ground and two mud-
spattered german boys struggling

to count to ten, then
vanishing into the mythical
mustard-yellow twilight, the horizon
sporting their spade like a flagpole.

GIERSCH

nicht zu unterschätzen: der giersch
mit dem begehren schon im namen – darum
die blüten, die so schwebend weiß sind, keusch
wie ein tyrannentraum.

kehrt stets zurück wie eine alte schuld,
schickt seine kassiber
durchs dunkel unterm rasen, unterm feld,
bis irgendwo erneut ein weißes wider-

standsnest emporschießt. hinter der garage,
beim knirschenden kies, der kirsche: giersch
als schäumen, als gischt, der ohne ein geräusch

geschieht, bis hoch zum giebel kriecht, bis giersch
schier überall sprießt, im ganzen garten giersch
sich über giersch schiebt, ihn verschlingt mit nichts als giersch.

BINDWEED

do not underestimate the bindweed,
its need for wreathe and stifle rooted deep
in its name – hence the blossom, blinding, white,
as chaste as a tyrant's dream.

like an ancient crime, an unpaid debt,
it returns to haunt a scene. by cover
of darkness, beneath the fields or a lawn,
it sends out feelers, fires a riot,

rises glorious in green. behind the barn,
convolved in cypress or bean, the unkind
climber spirals; a seething, creeping spume

it twines up walls and roan, choking
windows and drain, trumpeting, binding, abiding,
till nothing breathes but bindweed, and nothing more is seen.

VERSUCH ÜBER MÜCKEN

als hätten sich alle buchstaben
auf einmal aus der zeitung gelöst
und stünden als schwarm in der luft;

stehen als schwarm in der luft,
bringen von all den schlechten nachrichten
keine, dürftige musen, dürre

pegasusse, summen sich selbst nur ins ohr;
geschaffen aus dem letzten faden
von rauch, wenn die kerze erlischt,

so leicht, daß sich kaum sagen läßt: sie sind,
erscheinen sie fast als schatten,
die man aus einer anderen welt

in die unsere wirft; sie tanzen,
dünner als mit bleistift gezeichnet
die glieder; winzige sphinxenleiber;

der stein von rosetta, ohne den stein.

AN ESSAY ON MIDGES

as if all the letters had suddenly
floated free of a paper
and formed a swarm in the air;

they form a swarm in the air,
of all that bad news telling us
nothing, those skimpy muses, wispy

pegasuses, only abuzz with the hum
of themselves, made from the last twist
of smoke as the candle is snuffed,

so light you can hardly say: they are –
looking more like shadows, umbrae
jettisoned by another world

to enter our own, they dance, their legs
finer than anything pencil can draw,
with their miniscule sphinx-like bodies;

the rosetta stone, without the stone.

EIN PFERD

»*The well-aimed phrase is a whip*
your poem a horse.«
                  Michael Donaghy, nach Lu Chi

ist es ein fuchs, ein schimmel oder rappe,
hengst oder stute,
was durch den garten trabt und am rhabarber
zugange ist, an der lavendelstaude?

was dort über die triplebarre
hinwegsetzt, nur um in der mitte
des schlachtfelds zu landen, vor den karren
mit fässern und die goldene pyramide

aus heu gespannt? das kaltblut,
das aus brabant ein kiloschweres herz
heranschleppt und das V, den leichten pflug
der wildgänse, oder der lipizzaner, der als schwärze

geboren wird, der über alle felder
hinwegzutänzeln weiß und immer weißer,
der zum triumph wird, alle welt ins schach stellt,
blendend wie das schnupftuch eines kaisers?

versteht sich: sämtliche zweihundert-
undzweiundfünfzig knochen kannst du noch im schlaf
zusammensetzen, weißt vom huftritt,
erkenntnishart, der präzision im schweif,

den schemen, die sich nachts graubraun
am zaun der weide reiben, hü und brr,
hörst das erstickte wiehern in den gräbern
der pharaonen und eroberer.

A HORSE

> "The well-aimed phrase is a whip
> your poem a horse."
> MICHAEL DONAGHY, AFTER LU CHI

could it be chestnut, grey or black,
stallion or mare,
trotting through the garden to attack
the rhubarb stalks and lavender?

jumping the triple bar
only to land plumb in the middle
of the field of battle, hitched to a cart
loaded with barrels

and a golden pyramid of hay?
or a cart-horse heaving from brabant
its heavy heart and plough, a V
as light as a wild-goose flight, or lipizzan,

born dark and born to prance
through any terrain, pale as pierrot,
a triumph, holding the world in suspense,
radiant as an emperor's jabot?

and naturally you could assemble
its two-hundred and fifty-two bones in your sleep,
and you know its kick, as painful
as knowing oneself, the skilful whip

of their tails, dun shadows rubbing their skin
on the paddock fences at night, their whoa
and giddy-up, the smothered whinny
in the tomb of conqueror or pharaoh.

und doch bist du jetzt hier, rot wie ein bier-
kutscher und fluchend, mit dem zuckerstück
genialität in deiner tasche und dem tier,
das weder vor geht noch zurück,

nicht reagiert auf deine gerte
und auch nicht auf die möhre, die am band
vor seinen nüstern baumelt wie die kerze
vor der ikone. rühr dich, sagst du bebend.

es rührt sich nicht. es steht da, sieht ins land.

and yet here you are, as red in the face
as a cursing drayman, in your pocket
inspiration's sugar-lump, and this beast
that won't move forward, won't move back,

wholly ignoring your crop, unruffled,
unimpressed by the carrot you dangle
before its nose on a string, like a cand-
le held to an icon. budge! you beg, a-tremble.

it doesn't move. it stands. surveying the land.

DAS WEIDENKÄTZCHEN

warum sich tante mia wann genau
ein weidenkätzchen in die nase steckte,
verschweigt die geschichte. sicher ist: es wich,
je mehr sie es zu fassen suchte, stetig
zurück in seine dunkelheiten, weich
und weiß, ein hermelin in seinem bau.

der punkt, an dem die dinge sich entfernen;
der augenblick, in dem wir ignoriert
und nur noch zeuge sind oder statist,
bis jener teppich ruiniert,
der flügel aus dem zehnten stock gestürzt ist,
die ganze stadt ein flammendes inferno.

noch war krieg, doch sang die grille
trotz allem in den blühenden zweigen der weide,
im bach stand die mit licht gepanzerte
forelle. und nichts was half, keine pinzette
und keine stricknadel, bis man die schreiende kleine
in eine klinik brachte. dieser grelle

doppelmond der leuchte und der halo
von lachenden krankenschwestern über ihr –
fast möchte man mitlachen, wäre da nicht
der feine druck, der zwischen stirnhöhle
und nasenwurzel sitzt, hinterm gesicht,
der abwartet, beharrlich, wie ein tier.

THE CATKIN

what caused auntie mia to stick a catkin
up her nose, and when exactly she did,
our story cannot relate. what is for sure
is that the more she tried to entrap it
the further it retreated, its goal obscure,
so soft and white, an ermine in its den.

at what point do things begin to evade us,
how soon do we notice we do not count,
become mere witnesses or extras, before
that favourite carpet is ruined,
the grand piano plunges from the tenth floor,
our town has fallen and stands ablaze.

the war was not over, and yet the valiant
cricket sang on the blossoming willow spray,
and the trout, all armour-clad in sunlight,
hovered in the stream. but nothing helped,
neither pincette nor a needle, until they
took the wailing girl to hospital. radiant

then were the lamp's double moon, the halo
of laughing nurses over her head; to be fair
i might be laughing myself, it it weren't
for that subtle pressure behind the face – below
the sinus, beside the nasal cavity – bent
on sitting it out, like a beast in its lair.

GROTTENOLM

I

kaum wirklicher als das einhorn
und selten wie sphinx oder drache,
für dessen brut man ihn hielt,
als er sich erstmals zeigte, medusenhaupt
im spiegel eines baches;
schneeweißer fisch mit vier beinen,
wie die bauern ihn nannten,
dem schrei eines menschen.
seine kunst: vergessen zu werden.
so wird er alt. so überlebt er
die nach ihm suchen.

II

in einem reich ohne licht
und ohne farben, ohne wind,
sitzt der olm, der keine feinde
außer der sonne hat, zarter als die arbeit
von glasbläsern ist, kaum schwerer als ein brief
und leichter als ein schluck wasser.
weiß er nichts von unserer welt
oder weiß er alles? mit einer haut,
so durchlässig, daß sie nichts verwehrt
und alles aufnähme an giften,
an reichtümern, beschränkt er sich
aufs wenige, verzichtet aufs essen,
sogar auf den eigenen schatten.

OLM

I

hardly more real than the unicorn
and as rare as sphinx or dragon
whose offspring it was thought to be
when first it came to light, a medusa's head
in the mirror of a stream.
a snow-white fish with four legs
the country folk called it,
its cry like that of a human.
its skill: to be forgotten.
and so it grows old, and outlives
those who seek it.

II

in a realm without light
without colour, without wind,
you'll find the olm, who has no enemies
but the sun, is frailer than the work
of a glass-blower, little heavier than a letter
and lighter than a mouthful of water.
does it know nothing of our world
or does it know all? with a skin
so transparent that it blocks nothing
and would let all poisons through,
all treasures, it restricts itself
to a minimum, does without food,
even without its own shadow.

III

ich muß dir nahe-
gekommen sein, damals
hinter der grenze,
von der du nichts ahnst,
im karst, jener gegend,
in der noch immer
verschwinden kann,
wer spät in der nacht
zum rauchen hinausgeht
auf löchrigem grund,
hoch überm system
von grotten, wo rost
auf waffen lagert,
vielleicht gar soldaten
ergraut auf ein ende
des krieges warten,
jahrzehnte nach ende
des krieges, wo du,
geschmeidiges S,
durch leeren fliegst,
die dir sicher sind,
in päpstlichem weiß
durch höhlen, himmel,
kälterer bruder,
durch episches dunkel
mit nichts als der uhr
aus tropfendem wasser
und blind wie homer.

III

i must have been close
to you then, across
a border of which
you know nothing,
in the karst, a region
where even today,
one who goes out
for a smoke on the fissured
ground at night,
high above
the system of caves,
can easily go missing,
a place where rust
settles on weapons
and soldiers may wait
for the end of a war
that has ended decades
before, and where you,
lithesome S,
can fly through hollow
spaces in safety
in papal white,
through caves and heavens,
colder brother,
through epic darkness,
with nothing but the clock
of dripping water
and blind as homer.

LAKEN

großvater wurde einbalsamiert
in seines und hinausgetragen,
und ich entdeckte ihn ein jahr später,
als wir die betten frisch bezogen,
zur wespe verschrumpelt, winziger
pharao eines längst vergangenen sommers.

so faltete man laken: die arme
weit ausgebreitet, daß man sich zu spiegeln
begann über die straffgespannte fläche
hinweg; der wäschefoxtrott dann, bis schritt
um schritt ein rechteck im nächstkleineren
verschwand, bis sich die nasen fast berührten.

alles konnte verborgen sein
in ihrem schneeigen innern: ein leerer
flakon mit einem spuk parfum, ein paar
lavendelblüten oder wiesenblumen,
ein groschen oder ab und zu ein wurf
von mottenkugeln in seinem nest.

fürs erste aber ruhten sie, stumm
und weiß in ihren schränken, ganze
stapel von ihnen, eingelegt in duft,
gemangelt, gebügelt, gestärkt,
und sorgfältig gepackt wie fallschirme
vor einem sprung aus ungeahnten höhen.

SHEETS

grandfather was embalmed in his
and carried out, and i
discovered him one year
later when we changed the beds –
shrivelled to a wasp, tiny
pharaoh of a long-gone summer.

sheets were folded by spreading
your arms to mirror your opposite
across their taut expanse. then
came the laundry foxtrot: each
rectangle swallowed by its half,
our noses nearly touching.

anything could be hidden
in their snowy hearts: an empty
vial containing a ghost of perfume,
lavender blossoms or meadow
flowers, a penny, the odd
clutch of mothballs in their nest.

but now they slumbered, mute
and white in their cupboards, great
piles of them, steeped in fragrance,
mangled, ironed and starched,
as scrupulously stacked as parachutes
before a jump from undreamt-of heights.

IM BRUNNEN

sechs, sieben meter freier fall
und ich war weiter weg
als je zuvor, ein kosmonaut
in seiner kapsel aus feldstein,
betrachtete aus der ferne
das kostbare, runde blau.

ich war das kind
im brunnen. nur die moose
kletterten am geflochtenen
strick ihrer selbst nach oben,
efeu stieg über efeuschultern
ins freie, entkam.

ab und zu der weiße blitz
eines vogels, ab und zu
der weiße vogel blitz. ich aß,
was langsamer war. der mond,
der sich über die öffnung schob,
ein forscherauge überm mikroskop.

gerade, als ich die wörter assel und stein
als assel und stein zu begreifen lernte,
drang lärm herab, ein hasten, schreie,
und vor mir begann ein seil.

ich kehrte zurück ins läuten der glocken,
zurück zu brotgeruch und busfahrplänen,
dem schatten unter bäumen,
gesprächen übers wetter, kehrte
zurück zu taufen und tragödien,
den schlagzeilen, von denen
ich eine war.

IN THE WELL

six, seven metres free-fall
and i was further away
than ever before, a cosmonaut
in his field-stone capsule
gazing from afar
at the precious round of blue.

i was the child
in the well. only the moss
climbed the braided twine
of itself to the lip, ivy
climbed on shoulders of ivy
into the open to freedom.

now and then the white flash
of a bird, off and on
the white bird flash. i ate
anything slower. the moon
slid over the opening -
a boffin's eye at the microscope.

just when the words slater and stone
had begun to mean slater and stone,
noise arrived, a hollering and hurrying:
in front of my nose began a rope.

i went back to tolling bells,
back to bread-smells and bus times,
to shade under the trees
and talking about the weather, went
back to christenings and tragedies,
to the headlines, of which
i was one.

SELBSTPORTRÄT MIT BIENENSCHWARM

bis eben nichts als eine feine linie
um kinn und lippen, jetzt ein ganzer bart,
der wächst und wimmelt, bis ich magdalena
zu gleichen scheine, ganz und gar behaart

von bienen bin. wie es von allen seiten
heranstürmt, wie man langsam, gramm um gramm
an dasein zunimmt, an gewicht und weite,
das regungslose zentrum vom gesang…

ich ähnele mit meinen ausgestreck-
ten armen einem ritter, dem die knappen
in seine rüstung helfen, stück um stück,
erst helm, dann harnisch, arme, beine, nacken,

bis er sich kaum noch rühren kann, nicht läuft,
nur schimmernd dasteht, nur mit ein paar winden
hinter dem glanz, ein bißchen alter luft
und wirklich sichtbar erst mit dem verschwinden.

SELF-PORTRAIT WITH A SWARM OF BEES

a moment ago i wore at best a fuzz
around my chin and lips; but now my beard
is growing and seething i might even pass
for magdalena: all my face hirsute

with bees. how they come buzzing from every side,
and, ounce by ounce, how a person's being
slowly but steadily gains in weight and spread
to become the stone-still centre of song...

my arms outstretched i bear a resemblance
to some ancient knight whom bustling varlets help
to fit his suit of armour, piece by piece –
first the helmet, then the harness, arms, legs, nape,

until he can hardly move – who does not tread,
just stands there gleaming, with barely a hint
of wind behind the lustre, lingering breath,
and only vanishing becomes distinct.

BIOGRAPHICAL NOTES

JAN WAGNER is one of the most distinguished German poets of his generation. Born in Hamburg in 1971, he studied English in Hamburg, Dublin and Berlin, where he has lived since 1995. A poet, essayist and translator of British and American poetry (Charles Simic, Simon Armitage, Matthew Sweeney, Robin Robertson), he was also, until 2003, co-publisher of *Die Aussenseite des Elementes* (The Outside of the Element), a boxed loose-leaf periodical based on an idea by Marcel Duchamp. He has published six volumes of poetry, including *Probebohrung im Himmel* (Trial Drill in the Sky, 2001), *Guerickes Sperling* (Guericke's Sparrow, 2004), *Achtzehn Pasteten* (Eighteen Pastries, 2007) and, most recently, *Regentonnenvariationen* (Rain Barrel Variations, 2014). A selection of his essays, *Die Sandale des Propheten* (The Prophet's Sandal), appeared in 2011.

Jan Wagner has received numerous awards, including the Mondsee Poetry Award (2004), the Ernst Meister Prize for Poetry (2005), the Wilhelm Lehmann Prize (2009), the Friedrich Hölderlin Prize (2011) and the Mörike Preis (2015).

IAIN GALBRAITH studied Modern Languages and Comparative Literature at the universities of Cambridge, Freiburg and Mainz. He is a prolific translator of German and Austrian poetry, while his own poems have appeared in numerous anthologies and journals, including the *TLS*, *Poetry Review*, *PN Review*, *Warwick Review*, *Edinburgh Review* and *New Writing*. A winner of the John Dryden Translation Prize and the editor of five poetry anthologies, his recent translated books include a selection of W. G. Sebald's poetry, *Across the Land and the Water* (2011) and a 'Selected

Poems' of John Burnside in German, *Versuch über das Licht* (2011).

Besides translating poetry and fiction, Iain Galbraith is also a widely performed translator of British and Irish drama into German and a part-time lecturer in literary translation at the University of Applied Arts in Vienna. He grew up in the west of Scotland and lives in Wiesbaden, Germany.

He was the winner of the 2014 Stephen Spender Prize, awarded for his translation of Jan Wagner's poem 'Quince Jelly'.

KAREN LEEDER is a writer, translator and academic. Since 1993 she has taught German at New College, Oxford and is Professor of Modern German Literature there. She has published widely on modern German literature, especially poetry, including books on Brecht, Rilke and Durs Grünbein, as well as the contemporary German poetry scene. A book on lateness and modern poetry will appear in 2015. She is also a translator of German poetry into English, most recently Volker Braun, *Rubble Flora: Selected Poems*, with David Constantine and Michael Krüger, *Last Day of the Year: Selected Poems* (both 2014). Her translation of Evelyn Schlag's *Selected Poems* (2004) won the Schlegel Tieck Prize in 2005 and she won The Stephen Spender Prize in 2013 for her translation of Durs Grünbein.

Also available in the Arc Publications
'VISIBLE POETS' SERIES (Series Editor: Jean Boase-Beier)

No. 1 – MIKLÓS RADNÓTI (Hungary)
Camp Notebook
Translated by Francis Jones, introduced by George Szirtes

No. 2 – BARTOLO CATTAFI (Italy)
Anthracite
Translated by Brian Cole, introduced by Peter Dale
(Poetry Book Society Recommended Translation)

No. 3 – MICHAEL STRUNGE (Denmark)
A Virgin from a Chilly Decade
Translated by Bente Elsworth, introduced by John Fletcher

No. 4 – TADEUSZ RÓŻEWICZ (Poland)
recycling
Translated by Barbara Bogoczek (Plebanek) & Tony Howard,
introduced by Adam Czerniawski

No. 5 – CLAUDE DE BURINE (France)
Words Have Frozen Over
Translated by Martin Sorrell, introduced by Susan Wicks

No. 6 – CEVAT ÇAPAN (Turkey)
Where Are You, Susie Petschek?
Translated by Cevat Çapan & Michael Hulse,
introduced by A. S. Byatt

No. 7 – JEAN CASSOU (France)
33 Sonnets of the Resistance
With an original introduction by Louis Aragon
Translated by Timothy Adès, introduced by Alistair Elliot

No. 8 – ARJEN DUINKER (Holland)
The Sublime Song of a Maybe
Translated by Willem Groenewegen, introduced by Jeffrey Wainwright

No. 9 – MILA HAUGOVÁ (Slovakia)
Scent of the Unseen
Translated by James & Viera Sutherland-Smith,
introduced by Fiona Sampson

No. 10 – ERNST MEISTER (Germany)
Between Nothing and Nothing
Translated by Jean Boase-Beier, introduced by John Hartley Williams

No. 11 – YANNIS KONDOS (Greece)
Absurd Athlete
Translated by David Connolly, introduced by David Constantine

No. 12 – BEJAN MATUR (Turkey)
In the Temple of a Patient God
Translated by Ruth Christie, introduced by Maureen Freely

No. 13 – GABRIEL FERRATER (Catalonia / Spain)
Women and Days
Translated by Arthur Terry, introduced by Seamus Heaney

No. 14 – INNA LISNIANSKAYA (Russia)
Far from Sodom
Translated by Daniel Weissbort, introduced by Elaine Feinstein
(Poetry Book Society Recommended Translation)

No. 15 – SABINE LANGE (Germany)
The Fishermen Sleep
Translated by Jenny Williams, introduced by Mary O'Donnell

No. 16 – TAKAHASHI MUTSUO (Japan)
We of Zipangu
Translated by James Kirkup & Tamaki Makoto,
introduced by Glyn Pursglove

No. 17 – JURIS KRONBERGS (Latvia)
Wolf One-Eye
Translated by Mara Rozitis, introduced by Jaan Kaplinski

No. 18 – REMCO CAMPERT (Holland)
I Dreamed in the Cities at Night
Translated by Donald Gardner, introduced by Paul Vincent

No. 19 – DOROTHEA ROSA HERLIANY (Indonesia)
Kill the Radio
Translated by Harry Aveling, introduced by Linda France

No. 20 – SOLEÏMAN ADEL GUÉMAR (Algeria)
State of Emergency
Translated by Tom Cheesman & John Goodby,
introduced by Lisa Appignanesi
(PEN Translation Award)

No. 21 – ELI TOLARETXIPI (Spain / Basque)
Still Life with Loops
Translated by Philip Jenkins, introduced by Robert Crawford

No. 22 – FERNANDO KOFMAN (Argentina)
The Flights of Zarza
Translated by Ian Taylor, introduced by Andrew Graham Yooll

No. 23 – LARISSA MILLER (Russia)
Guests of Eternity
Translated by Richard McKane, introduced by Sasha Dugdale
(Poetry Book Society Recommended Translation)

No. 24 – ANISE KOLTZ (Luxembourg)
At the Edge of Night
Translated by Anne-Marie Glasheen, introduced by Caroline Price

No. 25 – MAURICE CARÊME (Belgium)
Defying Fate
Translated by Christopher Pilling, introduced by Martin Sorrell

No. 26 – VALÉRIE ROUZEAU (France)
Cold Spring in Winter
Translated by Susan Wicks, introduced by Stephen Romer
(Short-listed, Griffin Poetry Prize, 2010 &
Oxford-Weidenfeld Translation Prize, 2010)

No. 27 – RAZMIK DAVOYAN (France)
Whispers and Breath of the Meadows
Translated by Arminé Tamrazian, introduced by W. N. Herbert

No. 28 – FRANÇOIS JACQMIN (Belgium)
The Book of the Snow
Translated by Philip Mosley, introduced by Clive Scott
(Short-listed, Griffin Poetry Prize, 2011)

No. 29 – KRISTIINA EHIN (Estonia)
The Scent of Your Shadow
Translated by Ilmar Lehtpere, introduced by Sujata Bhatt
(Poetry Book Society Recommended Translation)

No. 30 – META KUŠAR (Slovenia)
Ljubljana
Translated by Ana Jelnikar & Stephen Watts,
introduced by Francis R. Jones

No. 31 – LUDWIG STEINHERR (Germany)
Before the Invention of Paradise
Translated by Richard Dove, introduced by Jean Boase-Beier

No. 32 – FABIO PUSTERLA (Switzerland)
Days Full of Caves and Tigers
Translated by Simon Knight, introduced by Alan Brownjohn

No. 33 – LEV LOSEFF (Russia)
As I Said
Translated by G.S. Smith, introduced by Barry P. Scherr

No. 34 – ANTONIO MOURA (Brazil)
Silence River
Translated by Stefan Tobler, introduced by David Treece

No. 35 – Birhan Keskin (Turkey)
& Silk & Love & Flame
Translated by George Messo, introduced by Amanda Dalton

No. 36 – Cheran (Sri Lanka)
In a Time of Burning
Translated by Lakshmi Holmström, introduced by Sascha Ebeling

No. 37 – Krystyna Miłobędzka (Poland)
Nothing More
Translated by Elżbieta Wójcik-Leese, introduced by Robert Minhinnick

No. 38 – Pedro Serrano (Mexico)
Peatlands
Translated by Anna Crowe, introduced by W. N. Herbert